KU-479-693

INTEGRATING RESEARCH

Applied Social Research Methods Series
Volume 2

INTEGRATING RESEARCH

A Guide for Literature Reviews

Second Edition

Harris M. Cooper

Applied Social Research Methods Series
Volume 2

SAGE PUBLICATIONS
The International Professional Publishers
Newbury Park   London   New Delhi

To Elizabeth

Copyright © 1989, 1984 by Sage Publications, Inc.

All rights reserved. No part of this book may be reproduced or utilized in any form or by any means, electronic or mechanical, including photocopying, recording, or by any information storage and retrieval system, without permission in writing from the publisher.

For information address:

SAGE Publications, Inc.
2455 Teller Road
Newbury Park, California 91320

SAGE Publications Ltd.
6 Bonhill Street
London EC2A 4PU
United Kingdom

SAGE Publications India Pvt. Ltd.
M-32 Market
Greater Kailash I
New Delhi 110 048 India

Printed in the United States of America

Library of Congress Cataloging-in-Publication Data

Cooper, Harris M.
    Integrating research.

    (Applied social research methods series ; v. 2)
    Rev. ed. of: The integrative research review /
Harris M. Cooper. c1984.
    Bibliography: p.
    Includes indexes.
    1. Social sciences—Research. I. Cooper, Harris M.
Integrative research review. II. Title. III. Title:
Literature reviews. IV. Series.
    H62.C5859 1989   300'.72   88-36233
    ISBN 0-8039-3430-0
    ISBN 0-8039-3431-9 (pbk.)

94 10 9

CONTENTS

PREFACE TO THE FIRST EDITION

Every research project in the social sciences should involve the inquirer searching out previous, related investigations. Without this step, an integrated, comprehensive picture of the world cannot be built. Researchers working in isolation repeat past mistakes and rarely achieve a sense of progress. Progress in social science comes from building on the efforts of those who have worked before.

Yet, the novice researcher has little guidance for how to conduct an integrative research review—how to find, evaluate, and synthesize previous research on the topic of interest. This book attempts to fill that void. It is intended for use by social science students with some background in basic research methods and statistics.

The approach to research reviewing espoused in this book represents a significant departure from how research reviews have been conducted in the past. Instead of the intuitive, subjective, narrative style that has been the traditional approach to research reviewing, this book presents a systematic, objective alternative. This approach is rapidly gaining acceptance in many social science fields. The reader learns how to carry out problem formulations, literature searches, research evaluations, and research syntheses according to rules based on scientific principles. The intended result is a replicable review that can create consensus among scholars and focus debate in a constructive fashion. Most important, users of this approach should finish their reviews feeling knowledgeable about the research area and confident that their future primary research can make a contribution to the field.

Several institutions and individuals were instrumental in the preparation of this book. First, the National Institute of Education provided research support while the manuscript was prepared. The grant, entitled "A systematic examination of the literature review and knowledge synthesis activities," was overseen by Spencer Ward of the NIE's Dissemination in Practice Program.

Special thanks go to four former graduate students: Maureen Findley, Ken Ottenbacher, David Tom, and Julie Yu. Each performed a research review in his or her own area of interest under my supervision. Their efforts have been used throughout the book to illustrate abstract points. While they were becoming expert in their fields, I was learning about problems in reviewing that transcend topic areas as well as about many more unique reviewing difficulties.

Jeanmarie Fraser, a librarian at the University of Missouri's Elmer Ellis Library, spent many hours conducting computerized literature searches for me and my students. She also graciously gave me a crash course in library science.

The first draft of this volume was read and critiqued by twelve people: Len Bickman, Ruth Haber, Larry Hedges, Ken Ottenbacher, Jolene Pettis, Ronald Ribble, Debra Rog, Robert Rosenthal, David Schumann, David Tom, Tedra

Walden, and Julie Yu. Each made comments that helped improve the final product.

Finally, the Center for Research in Social Behavior and especially its staff deserve my thanks. Patricia Shanks, Janice Meiburger, Terry Brown, and Diane Chappell transcribed, typed, and proofread the manuscript while tolerating a frenetic author. No simple task.

—*Harris Cooper*

PREFACE TO THE SECOND EDITION

In the years between editions of this book, scientific research reviewing changed from a controversial to an accepted practice. Its application is now found in every area of the social sciences; in some areas it is required.

The years have also brought improvements in integrative research reviewing techniques. Especially, the technology surrounding literature searching has improved. Also, the theoretical underpinnings of meta-analysis have been comprehensively described and the application of these procedures has been made more accessible.

This second edition incorporates these changes. In addition, two of the illustrations have been replaced with more up-to-date examples. Material on coding sheets and on the identification of independent hypothesis tests has been expanded. Finally, the tables needed to perform meta-analysis have been included in the text.

Even revisions require the help of others. Pamela Hazelrigg, a student of mine, coauthored one of the new illustrative reviews. Kathleen Connors, a reference librarian at the University of Oregon Library, helped update the sections on abstracting and indexing services. Larry Hedges again examined my exposition of statistical techniques. Cathy Luebbering typed, retyped, and proofread the manuscript. My thanks to these friends and colleagues.

—Harris Cooper

1

Introduction

This chapter presents a definition of the term *integrative research review*, a justification for critical attention to research reviews, and a five-stage research model for the reviewing process. The chapter also introduces four research reviews that serve as practical examples in the chapters that follow.

The pursuit of knowledge with the tools of science is a cooperative, interdependent process. The dozens or hundreds of hours spent conducting a scientific study ultimately contribute just one piece to an enormous puzzle. The value of any single study is derived as much from how it fits with and expands on previous work as from the study's intrinsic properties. Although it is true that some studies receive more attention than others, this is typically because the pieces of the puzzle they solve (or the puzzles they introduce) are extremely important, not because the studies are solutions in and of themselves.

THE NEED FOR ATTENTION TO
RESEARCH REVIEWS

Given the cumulative nature of science, trustworthy accounts of past research form a necessary condition for orderly knowledge building. Yet, research methods textbooks in the social sciences show a remarkable lack of attention to how an inquirer finds, evaluates, and integrates past research. This inattention is especially troubling today because the social sciences have recently undergone a huge increase in the amount of research being conducted. To accommodate the expanding demand for communication, the number of outlets for theoretical and research reports has burgeoned.

The ability to gain access to social science information has also changed dramatically in recent years. In particular, retrieval of past work has been facilitated by the computerized literature search. The computer's ability to scan abstracts rapidly has improved interested scientists' access to evidence, if they know how to use the technology.

Finally, the need for trustworthy accounts of past research is also strengthened by growing specialization within the social sciences. Time constraints make it impossible for most social scientists to keep abreast of primary research except within a few topic areas of special interest to them. Garvey and Griffith (1971) wrote about this situation in psychology:

The individual scientist is being overloaded with scientific information. Perhaps the alarm over an "information crisis" arose because sometime in the last information doubling period, the individual psychologist became overburdened and could no longer keep up with and assimilate all the information being produced that was related to his primary specialty. (p. 350)

GOALS AND PREMISES OF THE BOOK

The goal for this book is to compensate for the lack of attention given to the literature review in social science methods texts. It will apply the basic tenets of sound data gathering to a comprehensive synthesis of past research on a topic. The rules of rigorous, objective inquiry are the same whether the inquirer is conducting a primary study or a research review. The two types of inquiry, however, require techniques specific to their purpose, and the techniques for integrative research reviewing have largely been ignored in the past.

The underlying premise of this treatment is that *locating and integrating separate research projects involves inferences as central to the validity of knowledge as the inferences involved in primary data interpretation.* Due to the amount and diverse locations of social science information, the comprehensiveness and validity of review conclusions can no longer be taken for granted. A scientist performing a research review makes numerous decisions that affect the outcome of the review, and each choice may create threats to the outcome's trustworthiness. Therefore, if social science knowledge transmitted through research reviews is to be objective and believable, *research reviewers must be required to use the same rigorous methodology that is required of primary researchers.*

While substantial attention has been paid to validity issues in primary research (Bracht & Glass, 1968; Campbell, 1969; Campbell & Stanley, 1963; Cook & Campbell, 1979), the social sciences lack a conceptualization of the research review process that provides systematic guidelines for evaluating the validity of review outcomes. This book is an attempt to provide such an organizing scheme.

DEFINITIONS OF LITERATURE REVIEWS

Literature reviews typically appear as introductions to reports of new primary data or as more detailed independent works (e.g., Harper, Weins, & Matarazzo, 1978; Maccoby & Jacklin, 1974). The scope of a literature review that introduces new data is typically quite narrow. Research cited as an introduction to other primary research will be restricted to those studies pertinent to the specific issue addressed by the new data.

When a literature review appears independent of new data, it can serve decidedly broader purposes. A literature review can have numerous different focuses, goals, perspectives, coverage strategies, organizations, and audiences (Cooper, 1988). For instance, reviews can focus on research outcomes, research methods, theories, and/or applications. Reviews can attempt to integrate what others have done and said, to criticize previous scholarly works, to build bridges between related topic areas, and/or to identify the central issues in a field.

Reviews combining two sets of focuses and goals appear most frequently. The first type of literature review is the *integrative research review*. Integrative reviews summarize past research by drawing overall conclusions from many separate studies that are believed to address related or identical hypotheses. The integrative reviewer hopes to present the state of knowledge concerning the relation(s) of interest and to highlight important issues that research has left unresolved. From the reader's viewpoint, an integrative research review is intended to "replace those earlier papers that have been lost from sight behind the research front" (Price, 1965, p. 513), and to direct future research so that it yields a maximum amount of new information.

The second kind of literature review is a *theoretical review*. Here, the reviewer hopes to present the theories offered to explain a particular phenomenon and to compare them with regard to breadth, internal consistency, and the nature of their predictions. Theoretical reviews will typically contain descriptions of critical experiments already conducted or suggested, assessments of which theory is most powerful and consistent with known relations, and sometimes reformulations or integrations of abstract notions from different theories.

Often a comprehensive review will address several of these sets of issues. Integrative research reviews are most common, however, and theoretical reviews will typically contain some integrative review components. It is also not unusual for integrative reviews to address multiple, related hypotheses. For instance, a review might examine the relation between several different independent variables and a single dependent variable, or it might try to summarize research related to a series of temporally linked hypotheses.

The major emphasis of this book will be the integrative research review. Not only is this the most frequent kind of review, but it also contains all the decision points present in other reviews—and some unique points as well.

THE STAGES OF RESEARCH REVIEW

Most textbooks on research methodology suggest that scientific inquiry involves a temporally sequenced set of activities. Although methodologists differ in the subtlety of their definitions for research stages, the most important distinctions in stages can be identified with a gratifying degree of consensus. Methodologists also uniformly agree that the sequencing of stages is not fixed;

practicing researchers often skip over one or more stages and sometimes move backward as well as forward (Selltiz, Wrightsman, & Cook, 1976).

In this book, the process of integrative research reviewing will be conceptualized as containing five stages or phases: (1) problem formulation, (2) data collection, (3) evaluation of data points, (4) analysis and interpretation, and (5) presentation of results. Each stage of the review serves a function similar to the one it serves in primary data research. For example, in both primary research and research review the problem formulation stage involves the definition of variables, and the analysis and interpretation stage involves making a choice about what results are significant. Reviewers, like primary data collectors, can make different choices about how to carry out their inquiries. Differences in review methodologies will create variation in review conclusions. Most important, each methodological choice at each stage of a review may undermine the trustworthiness of the review's conclusion or, in more scientific terms, create a threat to the review's validity. (A more formal definition of *validity* appears in Chapter 4.)

The functions, sources of variance, and potential threats to validity associated with each stage of the review process are summarized in Figure 1.1. In the chapters that follow, each stage of the research review will be examined in greater detail.

Problem formulation stage. The first stage in the research process is the problem formulation stage. During problem formulation, the variables involved in the inquiry are given both abstract and concrete definitions. At this stage the researcher asks: "What operations are relevant to the concepts that concern the review?" More broadly, the researcher must decide what distinguishes relevant from irrelevant material.

In Chapter 2, the decision points encountered by a reviewer during the problem formulation stage are discussed. Included in this discussion will be answers to the following questions: (a) What affects a reviewer's decisions about the conceptual relevance of particular studies? (b) How should a reviewer handle hypotheses that involve the interaction of two or more independent variables? and (c) What role should past reviews play in formulating a problem? Chapter 2 will also present some concrete recommendations about what information a reviewer should collect from empirical studies that have been judged relevant to a problem area.

Data collection stage. The data collection stage of research involves making a choice about the population of elements that will be the focus of the study. Identifying populations for research reviews is complicated by the fact that the reviewer wants to make inferences about two targets. First, the reviewer wants the cumulative result of the review to be based on all previous research on the problem. Second, the reviewer hopes that the included studies will allow generalizations to the population of individuals (or other units) who are the focus of the topic area.

Figure 1.1: The Integrative Review Conceptualized as a Research Project

Stage Characteristics	Stage of Research				
	Problem Formulation	Data Collection	Data Evaluation	Analysis and Interpretation	Public Presentation
Research Question Asked	What evidence should be included in the review?	What procedures should be used to find relevant evidence?	What retrieved evidence should be included in the review?	What procedures should be used to make inferences about the literature as a whole?	What information should be included in the review report?
Primary Function in Review	Constructing definitions that distinguish relevant from irrelevant studies.	Determining which sources of potentially relevant studies to examine.	Applying criteria to separate "valid" from "invalid" studies.	Synthesizing valid retrieved studies.	Applying editorial criteria to separate important from unimportant information.
Procedural Differences That Create Variation in Review Conclusions	1. Differences in included operational definitions. 2. Differences in operational detail.	Differences in the research contained in sources of information.	1. Differences in quality criteria. 2. Differences in the influence of nonquality criteria.	Differences in rules of inference.	Differences in guidelines for editorial judgment.
Sources of Potential Invalidity in Review Conclusions	1. Narrow concepts might make review conclusions less definitive and robust. 2. Superficial operational detail might obscure interacting variables.	1. Accessed studies might be qualitatively different from the target population of studies. 2. People sampled in accessible studies might be different from target population of people.	1. Nonquality factors might cause improper weighting of study information. 2. Omissions in study reports might make conclusions unreliable.	1. Rules for distinguishing patterns from noise might be inappropriate. 2. Review-based evidence might be used to infer causality.	1. Omission of review procedures might make conclusions irreproducible. 2. Omission of review findings and study procedures might make conclusions obsolete.

SOURCE: Cooper, H., "Scientific guidelines for conducting integrative research reviews." *Review of Educational Research*, 1982, *52*, 291-302. Copyright 1982, American Educational Research Association, Washington, D.C. Reprinted by permission.

Chapter 3 presents a detailed discussion of methods for locating studies. The discussion includes a listing of the sources of studies available to social scientists, how to use the most important sources, and what biases may be present in the information contained in each source.

Data evaluation stage. After data are collected, the inquirer makes critical judgments about the quality of individual data points. Each data point is examined in light of surrounding evidence to determine whether it is contaminated by factors irrelevant to the problem under consideration.

Chapter 4 discusses how evaluations of research quality can be carried out and makes some suggestions concerning the assessment of interjudge reliability and where biases in judgments come from. Also, Chapter 4 contains some recommendations concerning unavailable research reports and reports that are incomplete.

Analysis and interpretation stage. During analysis and interpretation, the separate data points collected by the inquirer are synthesized into a unified statement about the research problem. Interpretation demands that the inquirer distinguish systematic data patterns from "noise" or chance fluctuation.

Chapter 5 contains an explanation of some methods for combining the results of separate studies and for estimating the size or magnitude of a relation. Some techniques for analyzing the difference in relation size found in different studies are also examined.

Public presentation stage. Creating a public document that describes the review is the task that completes a research endeavor. In Chapter 6, some concrete guidelines will be offered on how to report integrative research reviews.

FOUR ILLUSTRATIONS OF
RIGOROUS RESEARCH REVIEW

The best way to demonstrate both the feasibility and benefits of rigorous research reviewing is through example. For this reason, four research reviews have been chosen to illustrate the practical aspects of conducting rigorous integrative research reviews. The topics of the four reviews represent a broad spectrum of social science research, encompass qualitatively different kinds of research, and involve diverse conceptual and operational variables. Even though the topics are diverse, they are also general enough that readers in any discipline should find all four topics instructive and easy to follow without a large amount of background in the separate research areas. However, a brief introduction to each topic will be helpful.

The effect of homework on academic achievement (Cooper, 1989). Requiring students to carry out academic tasks during nonschool hours is a practice as old as formal schooling itself. However, the effectiveness of homework is still a source of controversy. Public opinion about homework has fluctuated throughout the twentieth century. Past summaries of the homework research have concluded that homework has positive effects or no effects, that the research was inconclusive, or that the effects of homework were mediated by too many circumstantial variables for any general conclusion to be drawn.

In examining the literature, this illustrative review uncovered ten different questions motivating homework research. Three dealt with the general issue of whether homework is effective and seven with variations in homework procedures (e.g., individualization, grading). The three hypotheses relating to homework's overall utility asked whether students doing homework outperformed students doing no homework or students doing in-class supervised study, or whether the amount of homework students do correlates with their achievement. For purposes of illustration, the results of research looking at only the first question will be examined: Do students doing homework achieve better than students receiving no homework and no alternative compensatory treatment?

Personality moderators of interpersonal expectancy effects in laboratory experiments (Cooper & Hazelrigg, 1988). One of the best established findings in social psychology is that the expectations one person holds for another can affect the other person's behavior. Empirical tests of interpersonal expectancy effects were first carried out in laboratory settings. Naive experimenters were led to believe photos of faces would receive either success or failure ratings from subjects when, in fact, identical photos were used in both conditions. Results revealed that experimenters who were expecting more successful ratings obtained more successful ratings from their subjects.

Realizing that not all people are equally susceptible to interpersonal expectancy effects, efforts were then undertaken to identify personality variables that might moderate the degree to which expectancies influence behavior. Five general hypotheses guided this research. Three hypotheses relate to the experimenter. They suggest that experimenters who have greater need to influence others, who are better encoders of nonverbal messages, and who make more favorable impressions on their subjects should produce more dramatic interpersonal expectancy effects. Two hypotheses relate to the subject. These suggest that subjects who are more acquiescent and who are better decoders of nonverbal messages ought to be more prone to behave in the way the experimenter expects. Cooper and Hazelrigg (1988) undertook the task of collecting and summarizing the research testing these five hypotheses.

Drug treatment of hyperactive children (Ottenbacher & Cooper, 1983). Hyperactivity, a disorder involving a deficit in attention, has been estimated to afflict between 4% and 20% of school-aged children. Due to its frequency, both educators and physicians have vigorously pursued effective treatments for hyperactivity. The proposed treatments range from dietary restrictions and supplements to behavior modification training. However, by far the most prevalent treatment of hyperactivity is pharmacological management; almost all children identified as hyperactive receive some form of drug therapy in the course of their treatment.

Although drug treatment of hyperactivity is so frequently prescribed, there is still substantial controversy over the advisability of its use. In addition, there has been some question about the relative effectiveness of different types of drugs (stimulants and nonstimulants) and about any drug's ability to affect behaviors beyond motor or perceptual performance (i.e., social adjustment and educational performance).

The research review undertaken by Ottenbacher and Cooper (1983) was intended to address three of these outstanding issues. Specifically, the primary questions the review was meant to answer were as follows: (a) What is the impact of the placebo effect on drug treatments of hyperactivity? (b) Do different drugs differ in their effect on hyperactivity? and (c) Is the effect of drug treatment generalizable to the social and educational behavior of hyperactive children?

Response rates to questionnaires (Yu & Cooper, 1983). One problem that plagues all the social sciences, and marketing research in particular, is nonresponse to survey questionnaires. When people are chosen for inclusion in a study but refuse or are unable to take part in it, the researcher must confront the possibility that the remaining sample is no longer representative of the target population.

Numerous techniques have been employed to maximize questionnaire response (Kanuk & Berensen, 1975), including preliminary notification that a questionnaire is coming, cover letters with different types of appeals, personalization of the request, inclusion of return envelopes and postage, monetary and nonmonetary incentives, and follow-up contacts. Past reviews of the effectiveness of these techniques have concluded that there was no strong support for the value of any technique other than the use of monetary incentives and follow-up contacts (Kanuk & Berensen, 1975). These reviews, however, were narrative syntheses of research.

Yu and Cooper (1983) attempted to go beyond past efforts by conducting a quantitative synthesis of the research literature. It was stated that because "response rates (or responses as a percent of the size of the contacted samples) are a universal measure of the effectiveness of a technique, the results [i.e., raw data] of studies which used the same technique [can be directly] arithmetically combined" (pp. 36-37). Conducting such an analysis was the purpose of this review.

EXERCISE

The best exercise to carry out while reading this book is to conduct an integrative research review in an area of interest to you. The review should attempt to apply the guidelines explicated in the chapters that follow. If such an exercise is not possible, try to conduct the more discrete exercises that appear at the end of each chapter. Often, these exercises can be further simplified by dividing the work among members of your class.

2

The Problem Formulation Stage

This chapter describes the process of formulating a hypothesis for guiding an integrative research review. Topics include the treatment of concepts and operations, the distinction between study-generated and review-generated evidence, the treatment of main effects and interactions, the role of previous reviews in new reviewing efforts, the development of coding sheets for primary research reports, and the threats to validity during problem formulation.

"No matter what problem you want to work on and no matter what method you will eventually use, your empirical work *must* begin with a careful consideration of the research problem" (Simon, 1978, p. 98). In its most basic form, the research problem includes the definition of variables and the rationale for relating the variables to one another. The rationale can be that a theory predicts a particular association between variables (as in confirmatory research) or that some other practical or intuitive consideration suggests that *any* discovered relation might be important (as in exploratory research). Either problem rationale can be used for undertaking primary research or a research review.

The choice of a relation to study in primary research is influenced by the interests of researchers and the social conditions that surround them (Selltiz et al., 1976). This holds true for the choice of a topic by prospective research reviewers as well, with an important restriction. Primary researchers are limited only by their imaginations, but research reviewers must study topics that already appear in the literature. In fact, a topic is probably not suitable for review unless it has appeared in the literature and has created appreciable interest within a discipline, either because the problem is of broad conceptual caliber or because it is surrounded by intense research activity.

The fact that reviews are tied to a finite universe of problems does not mean the activity of research synthesis is any less creative than primary research. Instead, the creativity in research review enters when reviewers are asked to make sense of many related but not identical theories or studies. More often than not, the cumulative results of studies are many times more complex than envisioned by the separate researchers who conducted them. The reviewer's instinct for uncovering variables that influence a relation and ability to generate divergent schemes are important ingredients in the research synthesis process.

DEFINITION OF VARIABLES
IN SCIENTIFIC INQUIRY

Similarities Between Primary Research and Research Review

The variables involved in a scientific inquiry must be defined in two ways. First, the variables must be given conceptual definitions. These describe qualities of the variables that are independent of time and space but that can be used to distinguish events that are and are not relevant to the concept (Carlsmith, Ellsworth, & Aronson, 1976). For instance, a conceptual definition of *achievement* might be "a person's level of academic functioning." Conceptual definitions can differ in abstractness, or in the number of events to which they refer. Thus if *achievement* is defined as "something gained through effort or exertion," the concept is more abstract than the first definition. The second definition would allow one to consider as achievement goals reached in social, physical, and political spheres, as well as academic ones. Both primary researchers and research reviewers must choose a conceptual definition and a degree of abstractness for their problem variables. Both must decide how likely it is that an event represents an instance of the variable of interest.

In order to relate concepts to concrete events, a variable must also be operationally defined. An operational definition is a set of instructions describing the observable events that allow one to determine if a concept is present in a particular situation (Reynolds, 1971). Thus an operational definition of an interpersonal expectancy effect might include "the difference between subjects' ratings of photos when the experimenter is expecting success ratings versus failure ratings." Again, both primary researchers and research reviewers must specify the operations included in their variable definitions.

Differences Between Primary Research and Research Review

Some differences between the two types of inquiry can also be found in variable definition. Primary researchers have little choice but to define their concepts operationally before the inquiry begins. Primary data collection cannot start until variables have been given some circumscribed empirical reality. An investigator of hyperactivity treatments must choose a drug and a dosage. Reviewers, on the other hand, need not be quite so theoretically rigorous. The literature search can begin with only a conceptual definition. The research reviewer has the comparative luxury of being able to evaluate the conceptual relevance of different operations as they appear in the literature (e.g., should after-school tutoring be considered homework?) or simultaneously with data collection. Of course, some a priori specification of operations is desirable and most reviewers do begin with empirical realizations in mind. It is not unusual, however, for reviewers to stumble upon operations that they did not initially consider but that, upon inspection, they decide are relevant to the construct. In sum, a primary researcher usually knows exactly what events constitute the domain to be sampled before data collection begins, but a reviewer may discover unanticipated samplings along the way.

A more significant distinction between the types of inquiry is that primary research typically involves only one (sometimes two) operational definition of the same construct. In contrast, research reviews usually involve many empirical realizations. Although no two participants are treated exactly alike in any single study, this variation will ordinarily be small compared to that introduced by the differences in laboratories, treatments, measurements, sampled population, and analysis techniques used in separate studies (see Light & Pillemer, 1984). The multiple operations contained in research reviews introduce a set of unique problems that need to be examined carefully.

MULTIPLE OPERATIONS IN
RESEARCH REVIEW

The "fit" between concepts and operations. Research reviewers undertaking the formulation of a problem must be aware of two potential incongruities that may arise because of the variety of operations in the literature. First, the reviewer anticipating multiple operations may begin a literature search with a broad problem definition but find that the operations used in previous relevant research have been quite narrow. For instance, the illustrative review of the relation between homework and achievement might have begun with a broad definition of achievement, including the academic, social, and physical spheres of behavior. If this were the case, the result would have been disappointing, since the vast majority of past research dealt only with achievement in academic matters. When such a circumstance arises, the reviewer must narrow the conceptual underpinnings of the review to be more congruent with operations. Otherwise, the conclusions of the review will appear more general than the data warrant.

The opposite problem, using narrow concepts defined by multiple broad measures, can also confront a reviewer. This would have occurred if the homework and achievement review had initially sought only academic measures of achievement but the literature search revealed many other types of achievement behavior. The reviewer then faces the choice of either broadening the concept or excluding many studies.

It is extremely important that a reviewer take care to reevaluate the correspondence between the level of abstractness of a concept definition and the representativeness of the operations that primary researchers have used to define it. While such redefinition of the problem as an inquiry proceeds is frowned upon in primary research, it appears that some flexibility may be necessary, if not beneficial, in research review.

Multiple operationism and concept-to-concept correspondence. Webb, Campbell, Schwartz, Sechrest, and Grove (1981) present strong arguments for the value of multiple operationism. They define *multiple operationism* as the use of many measures that supposedly share a theoretical concept "but have different patterns of irrelevant components" (p. 35). Multiple operationism has positive consequences because

> once a proposition has been confirmed by two or more independent measurement processes, the uncertainty of its interpretation is greatly reduced. . . . If a proposition can survive the onslaught of a series of imperfect measures, with all their irrelevant error, confidence should be placed in it. Of course, this confidence is increased by minimizing error in each instrument and by a reasonable belief in the different and divergent effects of the sources of error. (p. 35)

While Webb et al. (1981) hold out the potential for strengthened inferences due to multiple operations, their qualification must also be underscored. Multiple operationism can enhance concept-to-operation correspondence if all or most of the measures encompassed in the research review are of at least satisfactory validity. This reasoning is akin to the reasoning applied in classical measurement theory to the single items on a personality questionnaire. Small correlations between individual items (in this case operations) and a "true" score can add up to a reliable indicator *if* a sufficient number of minimally valid items (operations) are present. However, if the majority of operations bear no correspondence to the underlying concept or the operations share a different concept to a greater degree than they share the intended one, the conclusion of the review will be invalid regardless of how many items or operations are involved; this is also analogous to measurement theory.

The research reviewer also must examine research designs for threats to the correspondence of operations and concepts. If the research designs uncovered by a literature search contain the same invalidating procedures, then the correspondence between operations and concepts is threatened. The illustrative review of research concerning homework and achievement again provides a good example. Homework studies are conducted in naturally occurring classrooms. Because these studies are often conducted as theses or dissertations, they typically involve only a small sample of classrooms, with only one or two classrooms in the homework and no-homework conditions and with the teacher also being the experimenter. Therefore, the teacher can treat the students in the classes differently in ways other than whether or not he or she assigns homework. If all of the studies uncovered by the literature search were conducted by teachers teaching both conditions, then the rival hypothesis that differences in treatment other than homework might account for achievement differences could not be ruled out, no matter how many studies have been conducted. Luckily, studies were also conducted in which different teachers were randomly assigned to either homework or no-homework conditions or in which homework was manipulated within classrooms.

As another example, in the review of drug treatments of childhood hyperactivity, some studies were found that kept only physicians (those administering the treatment) blind as to whether they were giving a placebo or drug while other studies kept only recorders of the dependent variables blind. If results across both types of studies are similar, the possibility that expectancy effects explain the results is less plausible when the accumulated findings are examined.

In sum, then, the existence of multiple operations in research literatures presents the potential benefit of stronger inferences through "triangulation" of evidence. However, multiple operations do not ensure concept-to-operation correspondence if all or most of the measures lack minimal correspondence to the concept or if research designs all share a similar confounding of unintended influences with intended ones.

Substituting new concepts for old. Perhaps the most challenging circumstance in the social sciences occurs when a new concept is introduced to explain old findings. For example, in social psychology the notion of cognitive dissonance has been employed frequently to explain why an individual who was paid $1 to voice a counterattitudinal argument subsequently experiences greater attitude change than another person who was paid $25 to perform the same activity (Festinger & Carlsmith, 1959). Dissonance theory suggests that because the amount of money is not sufficient to justify the espousal of the counterattitudinal argument, the person feels discomfort that can be reduced only through a shift in attitude. However, Bem (1967) recast the results of these dissonance experiments by invoking a self-perception theory. Briefly, he speculated that participants who observe themselves espousing counterattitudinal arguments infer their opinions the same way an observer would. Participants who see themselves making an argument for $1 assume that because they are performing the behavior with little justification they must feel positive toward the attitude in question.

No matter how many replications of the $1/$25 experiment are uncovered, a research reviewer could not use the results to evaluate the correctness of the two theories. The research reviewer must take care to differentiate concepts and theories that predict similar and different results for the same set of operations. If predictions are different, the accumulated evidence can be used to evaluate the correctness of one theory or another, or the different circumstances in which each theory is correct. If, however, the theories make identical predictions, no comparative judgment based on research outcomes is possible.

The use of operations not originally related to the concept. Literature searches often uncover research that has been cast in a conceptual framework different from the reviewer's but that includes measures or manipulations relevant to the concepts the reviewer had in mind. For instance, there are several concepts similar to "hyperactivity" that appear in research. When relevant operations associated with different abstract constructs are identified, they most certainly should be considered for inclusion in the review. In fact, different concepts and theories behind similar operations can often be used to demonstrate the robustness of results. There is probably no better way to ensure that operations contain different patterns of irrelevant components than to have different researchers with different theoretical backgrounds perform related experiments.

The effects of multiple operations on review outcomes. Operational multiplicity does more than introduce potentially stronger inferences to conceptual variables. It is also the most important source of variance in the conclusions of different reviews meant to address the same topic. Operational multiplicity can affect review outcomes in two ways:

(1) *Variance in operational definitions.* The operational definitions used in two research reviews on the same topic can vary. As noted earlier, two reviewers using an identical label for an abstract concept can employ very different operational definitions or levels of abstraction. Each definition may contain some operations excluded by the other, or one reviewer's definition may completely contain the other.

(2) *Variance in operational detail.* Operational multiplicity also affects review outcomes by allowing reviewers to vary in their attention to methodological distinctions in the literature. This effect is attributable to differences in the way study operations are treated *after* the literature has been searched. Research reviewers, as Cook and Leviton (1981) note, "become detectives who use obtained data patterns as clues for generating potentially explanatory concepts that specify the conditions under which a positive, null, or negative relationship holds between two variables" (p. 462). Reviewers differ in how much detective work they undertake. Some reviewers may pay careful attention to study operations. They may decide to identify the operational and sample distinctions among retrieved studies meticulously. Other reviewers may feel that method- or participant-dependent relations are unlikely or they may simply use less care.

The illustrative reviews. Two of the four illustrative research reviews provide contrasting examples with regard to the broadness of their definitions, their fit between concepts and operations, and the impact of multiple operations on their findings.

The search for personality moderators of interpersonal expectancy effects uncovered 32 different scales used to measure experimenter personality and 27 scales used on subjects. There were 8 different scales used to measure the experimenter's need for social influence, 9 to measure expressiveness (encoding ability), and 11 to measure likability (4 measured constructs unrelated to the hypotheses). For subjects, 11 different scales were used to measure influenceability. Clearly, multiple operations have been used in this area. Thus, because multiple operations were used, it is fairly certain that other personality variables confounded with any single scale had little effect on the review's conclusions regarding these four hypotheses. However, while the broad hypotheses may appear to be covered by the multiple scales, nearly all of the measures were of the paper-and-pencil variety. Therefore, we must still entertain the possibility that confounds associated with paper-and-pencil tests in general (like the social desirability of answers and evaluation apprehension) may still be confounded in the review's results.

With regard to measures of the effect of interpersonal expectancies, four different operationalizations were used. The simplest was to use raw score photo ratings and enter the expectancy condition (success or failure) into an analysis of variance along with the personality dimension. Other procedures defined expectancy effects by looking at the discrepancy between the expected and obtained ratings. These measures differ not only in how they are calculated but also in whether they define an expectancy effect by the extremity of the obtained rating or by the accuracy with which the obtained rating reflects the expectation—two very different conceptualizations.

The review involving the effects of research design on questionnaire response rates presented the least difficulty with regard to problem formulation. The dependent variable, response rates to questionnaires, was identical across all studies. This is an instance in which very narrow conceptual and operational definitions are perfectly commensurate with the review's objectives. Similarly, the research designs covered by the review were all operationally defined. Thus, although about two dozen different research designs were examined (e.g., cover letters, monetary incentives), there was no need to propose an overarching conceptual variable to encompass them all (other than "research design," of course).

JUDGING THE
CONCEPTUAL RELEVANCE OF STUDIES

In presenting the operations included in two illustrative reviews and relating these to the reviewers' abstract notions, a more fundamental question was sidestepped: How were studies judged to be conceptually relevant in the first place? The rules the reviewer uses to distinguish relevant from irrelevant studies determine the degree of "fit" between concepts and operations.

Information scientists have closely scrutinized the question of what makes a study relevant to a research problem (Saracevic, 1970). Regrettably, the degree of concept abstractness that a reviewer employs has not been examined as an influence on the relevance judgment. It has been shown, however, that judgments about the relevance of studies to a literature search are related to a reviewer's open-mindedness and expertise in the area (Davidson, 1977), whether the decision is based on titles or abstracts (Cooper & Ribble, in press), and even the amount of time the reviewer has for making relevance decisions (Cuadra & Katter, 1967). Thus, while the conceptual definition and level of abstractness that a reviewer chooses for a problem are certainly two influences on the studies deemed relevant, a multitude of other factors also affect this screening of information.

The only general recommendation that can be made with regard to conceptual relevance is that the reviewer should begin the literature search with the broadest conceptual definition in mind. In determining the acceptability of operations for inclusion within the broad concept, the reviewer again should remain as open-minded as possible. At later stages in the review—notably, during data evaluation—it is possible for a reviewer to exclude particular operations due to their lack of relevance or impurity. In the problem formulation and search stages, however, the reviewer should err on the overly inclusive side, just as a primary researcher collects some data that might not be used in analysis. It is most distressing to find out *after* studies have been retrieved and catalogued that available pieces of the puzzle were passed over and that the search must be reconstituted.

The broader search also allows the reviewer to undertake a review with greater operational detail. The benefits of broad conceptualization are underscored many times in the chapters that follow.

The illustrative reviews. The review of the effectiveness of homework faced several problems concerning whether or not to include certain kinds of operations. Behavior therapists often assign their clients "homework," or exercises meant to help them overcome phobias. A broad conceptualization might include this type of homework. Closer to the usual school-related meaning, some students often receive tutoring after school hours. Others take study-at-home television or videocassette courses. Some ways to define the concept of homework might include all or any of these activities. Ultimately, the decision was made to exclude these types of activities by defining *homework* as "tasks assigned to students by schoolteachers that are meant to be carried out during nonschool hours."

The drug treatments and response rate reviews presented few cases in which studies were difficult to classify as relevant or irrelevant, because the narrow objectives of these reviews meant there was little variation in method from one relevant study to another.

RELATIONS BETWEEN DIFFERENT CONCEPTS
IN RESEARCH REVIEWS

The problems that motivate most research reviews initially involve relations between two variables. There is a simple explanation for this: Main effects have typically been tested more often than any given interaction involving the same three variables. Three of the four research reviews serving as illustrations took a bivariate relation as their initial focus. These reviews, however, also examined potential influences on the main effect relation. One review, looking at personality moderators of interpersonal expectancy effects, began by examining three-variable relations. The main effect involved the impact of expectancies on social judgments, but the relation of interest involved how this main effect was influenced by the personality of the expectant person and target.

While some specific interactional hypotheses in the social sciences have generated enough interest to require independent research review, for the vast majority of topics the initial problem formulation will involve a main effect question. Again, however, the initial undertaking of the review to establish the existence of a main effect should in no way diminish the reviewer's attention to the interactive or moderating influences that may be discovered. If main effect relations are found to be moderated by third variables, these findings have inferential priority. Even when an interaction is the primary focus, the search for higher-order interactions should continue. Thus the review of personality moderators looked at whether these interaction effects were more or less likely to appear under different circumstances, including the presence of incentives for the experimenter to obtain expectancy effects and the degree of ambiguity in the photos. More will be said on the relations between variables in Chapter 5, which discusses how main effects and interactions are interpreted in research reviews.

STUDY-GENERATED AND REVIEW-GENERATED EVIDENCE

There are two different sources of evidence about relations contained in research reviews. The first type is called *study-generated evidence*. Specifically, study-generated evidence is present when a single study contains results that directly test the relation being considered. Research reviews also contain evidence that does not come from individual studies, but rather from the variations in procedures across studies. This type of evidence, called *review-generated evidence*, is present when the results of studies using different procedures to test the same hypothesis are compared to one another.

Any relation can be examined through either study- or review-generated evidence, but only study-generated evidence allows the reviewer to make statements concerning causality. An example will clarify the point. With regard to hyperactivity studies, suppose a reviewer is interested in whether stimulants and nonstimulants have different effects on hyperactivity. Suppose also that 16 studies are found that randomly assigned children to stimulant or nonstimulant experimental conditions. The accumulated results of these studies could then be interpreted as supporting or not supporting the idea that different drugs cause different effects on hyperactivity. Now assume that the reviewer uncovered 8 studies that employed only stimulant drugs tested against no-drug control groups and 8 other studies that compared only nonstimulant drugs with no-drug controls. If this review-generated evidence revealed a diminution in hyperactivity in the stimulant drug studies but not in the nonstimulant drug studies, then an association, but not a causal relation, could be inferred.

Why is this the case? Causal direction is not the problem with review-generated evidence. It would be foolish to argue that the amount of change in hyperactivity experienced by children caused the experimenters' choice of a drug. However, another ingredient of causality, the absence of potential third variables causing the relation, or nonspuriousness, is problematic. A multitude of third variables are potentially confounded with the original experimenter's choice of a stimulant or a nonstimulant drug. For instance, the experimenters who used nonstimulant drugs may also have employed different means for assessing hyperactivity. Or experimenters who are interested in studying children with different severities or types of hyperactivity may also choose to study different drugs. If the number of studies showing different results is large, it may be difficult to find other design characteristics confounded with the researchers' choice of what drug to use, but it is still possible. Therefore, review-generated evidence cannot legitimately rule out variables confounded with the study characteristic of interest as possible true causes. Spuriousness cannot be eliminated because the reviewer did not randomly assign drugs to experiments! In primary research it is this random assignment that allows us to assume third variables are represented equally in the experimental conditions.

The above example illustrates how review-generated evidence is typically used to examine potential moderators of relations. As in this example, most review-generated evidence examines interactional hypotheses, or the effect of a third variable on the strength or direction of a relation. It is often quite difficult to test main effect relations with review-generated evidence because social scientists use different scales to measure their dependent variables, even within a topic area. The problem of nonstandard measurements is circumvented when study characteristics are tested as *third* variables because the main effect relations *within* the studies can be transformed into standard effect size estimates, thus controlling for different scales (see Chapter 5).

One example of how main effect relations can be tested through review-generated evidence, however, is contained in the illustrative review of research design effects on response rates. In this review, studies were identified in which a particular design characteristic—say, the employment of a monetary incentive—was experimentally manipulated by the primary researchers. That is, in some studies a randomly chosen subsample of potential respondents was given a monetary incentive and another subsample was not give an incentive. This is study-generated evidence on a main effect hypothesis. However, the reviewers were also able to locate studies that explicitly stated that *all* respondents received a monetary incentive or that *no* respondents received a monetary incentive. Because the dependent variables used in these studies were identical (i.e., response rates), it was possible to compare the response rates in these separate studies with one another, thus testing a main effect relation with review-generated evidence. The study-generated evidence comparing monetary incentive and no-incentive conditions could tell whether monetary incentives caused a difference in response rates. Such information could then be supplemented by examining the response rates in studies without an incentive and studies with an incentive. The second source of evidence could not stand alone as the basis of causal inferences, however.

It is important, then, for reviewers to keep the distinction between study-generated and review-generated evidence in mind. Only evidence coming from experimental manipulations within a single study can support assertions concerning causality. But the lesser status of review-generated evidence with regard to causal inferences does not mean this evidential base should be ignored.

The use of review-generated evidence allows the reviewer to test relations that may have never been examined by primary researchers. Even though this evidence is equivocal, it is a major benefit of research reviewing and a source of potential hypotheses for future primary research.

THE ROLE OF PAST REVIEWS

If the topic of a review has a long history of interest within a discipline, it is likely that a reviewer attempting to use the guidelines set forth in this book will find that relevant reviews already exist. Obviously, these efforts need to be scrutinized carefully before the new review is undertaken. Past reviews can help establish the necessity of a new review. This assessment process is much like that used in primary research before a researcher undertakes a new study.

There are several things a new reviewer can look for in past reviews. First, past reviews can be employed to identify the positions of other scholars in the field. In particular, past reviews can be used to determine whether conflicting conclusions exist about the evidence and, if they do, what has caused the conflict.

Second, one can review past reviews to assess the earlier efforts' completeness and validity. As a demonstration of the benefits of using quantitative procedures in reviews, I compared a statistical review of research on gender differences in conformity to a traditional review (Maccoby & Jacklin, 1974). Using the same studies employed by the narrative reviewers, I was able to demonstrate that the narrative review's conclusions were somewhat conservative in light of the evidence the authors uncovered (see Cooper, 1979).

Past reviews can also be a significant help in identifying interacting variables that the new reviewer might wish to examine. Rather than restart the compilation of potential moderating variables, past reviewers will undoubtedly offer many suggestions based on previous efforts and their own intellect. If more than one review of an area has been conducted, the new review will be able to incorporate all of the suggestions.

Finally, past reviews allow the researcher to begin the compilation of a relevant bibliography. Most reviews have fairly lengthy bibliographies. If more than one review exists, the citations will usually overlap somewhat, but they may also be quite distinct. As an example, Findley and Cooper (1981) found that the research cited under the same chapter titles in introductory social psychology textbooks differed substantially. Along with the techniques described in the next chapter, the research cited in past reviews provides an excellent place for the new reviewer to start the literature search.

The illustrative reviews. Of the four illustrative reviews, the review of homework research is the one that best demonstrates the use of past reviews. Nine previous independent reviews were located that made statements about whether or not homework affected academic achievement. Given that nine past reviews existed, it was necessary to justify the need for yet a tenth review. First, it was shown that the nine reviews differed dramatically in their general conclusions concerning homework's effectiveness. Second, different reviews examined different sets of variables posited as moderators of homework's effects. Third, when the same moderators were examined, different reviewers sometimes drew opposite conclusions about their effects. Fourth, it was found that none of the past reviews was very comprehensive—no single review included more than 60% of the total research base uncovered by all the reviewers. Therefore, the new review could be used to resolve conflicts among previous reviews, to examine all at once the proposed moderators of homework's effects, and to include a more comprehensive research base. It was not claimed, however, that the past reviews were of no use—they helped in the development of a conceptual framework for describing the homework process, laid out issues that needed to be addressed when the effects of homework were assessed, and suggested a comprehensive catalog of contextual factors that might influence the utility of home study.

THE RESEARCH REVIEW CODING SHEET

Once the reviewer has formulated the problem and has an idea about what theorists, primary researchers, and past reviewers have said on the topic, the next step is to construct a coding sheet. The coding sheet is used to collect information from the primary research reports. If the number of studies involved in the research review is small, it may not be necessary for the reviewer to have a well-formulated idea about what information to extract from reports before the literature search begins. If only a dozen or so relevant articles exist, the reviewer can retrieve them in their entirety and read and reread them until he or she has gleaned the needed information. Small sets of studies allow the reviewer to follow up interesting ideas that emerge after he or she has read several studies by returning briefly to those previously scrutinized. However, if the reviewer expects to uncover a large amount of research, such a rereading of reports may be prohibitively time-consuming. In this instance, it is necessary for the reviewer to consider carefully what data will be retrieved from each research report before the formal search begins. It is important to pilot test this expectation against a few research reports and to modify the coding sheet so that a fairly standard and thorough examination of each research report can be conducted in a single reading. The rules for constructing a coding sheet are similar to those used in creating a coding frame and data matrix for a primary research effort (see Selltiz et al., 1976).

The first rule in constructing a review coding sheet is that any information that might have the remotest possibility of being considered relevant to the research review should be retrieved from the studies. Once the literature search has begun, it is exceedingly difficult to re-retrieve new information from studies that have already been coded. It is much less of a problem to include information that will not be used.

Information to include on the coding sheet. There are certain pieces of information about primary research that every reviewer will want to include on a research review coding sheet.

First, the reviewer will want to retrieve information concerning the background characteristics of the research report itself: the authors of the report, the source of the report, when the report was published, and what information channel led to the report's discovery.

The reviewer will also want to retrieve information concerning the research design of the primary studies. The particular design characteristics of interest will vary from topic to topic. A comprehensive discussion of research designs and their interpretation can be found in Cook and Campbell (1979). Most research designs, however, are covered by five categories: one-group pretest-posttest, correlational, nonequivalent control group (i.e., treatments are given to groups that existed before the research began), nonequivalent control group with matching or statistical control (i.e., some procedure was used to enhance the equivalence of intact groups), and random assignment to treatments. In some instances this categorization will suffice, but in others different designs will need to be added (e.g., time series) or finer distinctions made in the designs described above (e.g., distinctions between different matching or statistical control procedures).

Other features of research design may also be relevant. These might include whether or not repeated measures and/or counterbalancing of treatments was used, and the presence or absence of controls against experimenter bias.

In addition to basic research design issues, the reviewer will need to describe carefully the details that went into manipulating or measuring the independent variable. What was the nature of the treatment? Did it vary in intensity and duration from study to study? Were manipulation checks taken and, if so, what did they reveal?

Equally important are characteristics of how control or comparison groups were treated. Was there an alternate treatment? If so, what was it? If not, what did control groups do or how were they obtained? Differences among studies on any of these variables would be prime candidates for causes of differences in study outcomes.

For studies involving personality or other multi-item scales, the reviewer will want to retrieve information concerning the names of the tests, whether or not they were standardized, the number of items they included, and the tests' reliability, if this information is available. Similar information on the dependent variables used in experimental studies also needs to be cataloged carefully. While experimental dependent variables are often answers to single questions or discrete behaviors, they too can vary in important ways from study to study—for example, in their reactivity, sensitivity, or the length of delay before they are measured.

Another area of information needed in most reviews involves the characteristics of the participants included in the primary research. It is clearly important to retrieve the number of participants in each condition of the study. The reviewer will also want to retrieve information concerning the location and age of participants as well as any restrictions on participant populations that were employed.

Research review coding sheets should also contain information on the outcomes of the study. First and most important, the coding sheet needs to identify the direction of outcomes of comparisons. Was the hypothesis supported or refuted and what was the level of significance associated with the hypothesis test?

If a quantitative synthesis of results is envisioned, the reviewer will also need to record more precise information on the statistical outcomes of studies. Because reporting of results varies from article to article and can take several different forms, it is possible to list the statistical outcomes of studies in terms of how desirable they are for use in quantitative synthesis. Listed from most to least desirable, these would be as follows:

(1) the means, standard deviations, and sample sizes for each group in a comparison or hypothesis test;

(2) an estimate of the treatment's impact or the association between variables (e.g., correlation coefficient);

(3) the exact value of an inference test statistic and its associated degrees of freedom; and

(4) an inexact p-level and sample size.

Means and standard deviations allow the reviewer to calculate any effect sizes precisely for whatever comparisons he or she chooses. Effect sizes calculated by the primary researchers, while an excellent source of information, may contain unknown errors and may not be in the metric chosen by the reviewer. Values of inference test statistics and degrees of freedom allow the reviewer to estimate effect sizes, and inexact p-levels along with sample sizes allow the estimation of inference test values. The inference test values and p-levels also sometimes refer to analyses containing multiple factors (e.g., analysis of variance with more than one independent variable) and, unless these factors are the same across studies, this will add to the imprecision in estimates. Many issues involved in the extraction of statistical information from research reports will be discussed further in the chapters that follow.

Finally, each study report will also contain some miscellaneous but important design characteristics or results that the reviewer will want to note on the coding sheet. In many instances, the coding sheet will be standardized to accommodate information about the main effect comparison of interest, but the research report will contain evidence concerning interactions between the main effect and other variables. Therefore, the coding sheet should contain space for noting the number of variables employed in a design or analysis and the outcomes of any interaction tests that involved the relation of interest.

Low- and high-inference codings. The categories listed above might all be thought of as "low-inference" codings. That is, they require the coder only to locate the needed information in the research report and transfer it to the coding sheet. In other circumstances, coders might be asked to make some inferential judgments about the studies. These judgments often involve coders' attempts to infer how an experimental manipulation might have been interpreted by subjects. A review by Carlson and Miller (1987) provides a good example. These authors were summarizing the literature on why negative mood states seem to enhance the likelihood that people will lend a helping hand. In order to test different interpretations of this research, they needed to estimate how sad, guilty, angry, or frustrated different experimental procedures might have made subjects. To do this, they asked coders to read excerpts from the methods sections of relevant articles. The coders then used a 1-to-9 scale to rate, for example, the "extent to which subjects feel specifically downcast, sad, or depressed as a result of the negative-mood induction" (p. 96).

These "high-inference" codings create a special set of problems for research reviewers. First, careful attention must be paid to the reliability of high-inference coder judgments. Also, in these situations, coders are being asked to play the role of a research subject, and the validity of role-playing methodologies has been the source of much controversy (Greenberg & Folger, 1988). However, high-inference codings potentially add a new dimension to research reviewers' ability to interpret literatures and resolve controversies. If reviewers feel they can validly extract high-inference codes from articles and persuasively explain their rationale for doing so, then this technique deserves a try.

Revising and pilot testing the coding sheet. When an area of research is large and complex, the construction of a coding sheet can be a difficult task. In the process of devising categories, reviewers makes crucial decisions about what the important issues are in a field. Often, reviewers find that ideas they have about a topic and its research are only vague impressions. The coding sheet forces them to be more precise in their thinking.

The first draft of a coding sheet should never be the last. Reviewers need to show a first draft to knowledgeable colleagues for their input, and then code a few randomly selected studies using the coding sheet. They can then add categories and define category descriptors more precisely. Finally, they should have different coders pilot test the coding sheet to uncover any remaining ambiguities. This process shouldn't be viewed as a nuisance, but as an intrinsic part of problem formulation. The development of a coding sheet should be viewed as no less important to the success of a research review than the construction of a questionnaire is to survey research or an observation scheme to a study of naturalistic behavior.

Finally, a general coding sheet will never capture the unique aspects of all studies. Completed coding sheets often contain many blank spaces and notes in the margins. Perfection is never achieved. The reviewer can view these occurrences as failures (which they are not) or as targets for opportunity, highlighting the diversity of research in the topic area.

The illustrative reviews. The coding sheet for the review on the effects of homework is reproduced in Figure 2.1. The rationale behind most of the categories is self-evident, but an explanation concerning some decisions about what information to retrieve may prove instructive.

The section on research design contains no category for correlational studies, even though such a category was recommended above. This is because studies that used correlational designs invariably examined the amount of time students reported spending on homework as a continuous variable. An entirely different coding sheet was devised for these studies. They engendered a unique set of issues, including how samples of students were drawn from larger populations and whether teachers, students, or parents reported how much time the student spent on homework. There were also several of the categories in Figure 2.1 that were irrelevant to time-on-homework studies, such as the sections on research design and on the reporting of means and standard deviations.

There is no section in Figure 2.1 for delineating how the control group was treated. This is because all control groups used in these comparisons were treated identically—they received no treatment at all.

The homework coding sheet asked for a bit more detail regarding nonequivalent control group and random assignment designs than was suggested above. When a nonequivalent control group was used with a matching procedure, coders were asked to distinguish between matching based on (a) a pretest using the same measure as the dependent variable or (b) other variables related but not identical to the dependent variable. It was felt that the two procedures might differ in their ability to produce equivalent groups and therefore might explain differences in the outcomes of studies. For a similar reason a distinction was made among studies randomly assigning individual students or whole classrooms to homework and no-homework treatments.

It should be pointed out that much of the information asked for on the coding sheet was never actually examined in the completed review. This was true of all the information about students other than grade level. In these cases either too few studies reported information about the variable of interest (e.g., socioeconomic status of the students) or it was found that studies did not vary enough to allow valid inferences (e.g., comparing studies done in public and private schools).

Each of the coding sheets was designed to contain information concerning a single comparison. However, in some studies comparisons were reported for, say, more than one grade level or more than one dependent variable. When such a study was uncovered, the coder would fill out separate sheets for each two-group comparison. For example, a study with both standardized achievement and class grade measures reported separately for students in fifth and seventh grades would have four coding sheets associated with it. A more detailed discussion of how to handle multiple comparisons from the same study will be presented in Chapter 4.

VALIDITY ISSUES IN PROBLEM FORMULATION

Although, as has been noted, several decisions made during problem formulation can affect the validity of a research review, the two most central involve the notions of conceptual breadth and operational detail.

Author(s)_____

Title_____

Journal_____

Year_____ Volume_____ Pages_____

Source of Reference

Design (check one):

        One group pretest-posttest___   Random assignment___
        Nonequivalent control group___   of students___
           no matching___   of classrooms___
           matching on pretest___
           statistical control___

Other Design Features:

        Repeated measures   yes___ no___
        Counterbalancing   yes___ no___
        Teacher as experimenter yes___ no___

Sample Size:

        # of schools_____
        # of classrooms_____
        # of students_____

School Variables:

        Location _____ (use state abbreviations)
        Source of funding: public___ private___

Student Variables:

        Grade level(s)____
        SES: lower___ middle___ upper___
        Race: white___ black___ other___ random sample or mixed___
        Ability level: low___ average___ high___

Subject Matter (check all that apply):

        Math___   Social Studies___
          computation___   Science___
          problem solving___   Other (specify)_____
          concept formation___
        Reading___
        Writing/Spelling___
        Language/Vocabulary___

Figure 2.1: Coding Sheet for Homework Versus No-Treatment Studies

First, reviewers who use only a few operational definitions in their reviews typically do so to ensure consensus about how their concepts are related to operations. Such agreement is an attractive scientific goal. However, most methodologists agree that multiple realizations of concepts are desirable. As stated above, if multiple operations produce similar results, numerous rival interpretations for the findings may be ruled out. Also, narrow conceptualizations provide little information about the generality or robustness of results.

```
Homework Treatment:

    Weeks of treatment___
    Frequency of assignments per week___
    Average length of assignments___

Dependent Variable:

    Standard test (specify)_____
    Class grade_____
    Comprehensive tests (teacher-constructed)___
    Unit test___
    Attitude___

Statistical Outcome:

    Homework    M _____ sd _____ n _____
    No homework M _____ sd _____ n _____
    Type of inference test F___ t___ Chi___ Other _____
    Test value _____
    df _____
    p-level _____
    Effect size _____

Other Statistical Information:

    Other variables in analyses (list)
    _____
    _____
    _____


    Significant interactions involving homework
    variable _____ test value _____ df _____
    variable _____ test value _____ df _____
    variable _____ test value _____ df _____

Notes and comments:
```

Figure 2.1 continued

Therefore, the greater the conceptual breadth of a review, the greater its *potential* to produce conclusions that are more general than those from reviews using narrow definitions.

The word *potential* is emphasized because of the second threat to validity associated with the problem definition stage of review. If a reviewer details study operations only cursorily, the review conclusions may mask important distinctions in results. As Presby (1978) notes, "Differences [in studies] are cancelled in the use of very broad categories, which leads to the erroneous conclusion that research results indicate negligible differences in outcomes" (p. 514).

Of course, the most extreme attention to operational detail occurs when each study is treated as if it tested a completely different hypothesis. However, it is rare for a reviewer to conclude that no integration of the literature is possible due to the variation in methods across studies. Therefore, most reviews contain some threat to validity from ignoring methodological differences among studies, but the risk occurs in varying degrees in different reviews.

A lack of overlap in the operational definitions considered relevant by different reviews was not mentioned as a threat to validity, although it does create variance in review conclusions. This cannot be called a "threat," because it is impossible to say which of two reviews is more valid if the reviewers disagree about the operationalization of the same construct. Reviews that do not overlap in operations are not comparable on any level but the definitional one. On the other hand, it seems clear that a review that includes all the operations contained in another review plus additional operations is the more desirable review—if operational details receive appropriate treatment, of course. In practice, comparative evaluations will not be as clear-cut as these examples. Two reviews involving the same concept may share some operations while each also includes operations the other does not.

Protecting validity. Reviewers can use the following guidelines to protect their conclusions from threats to validity entering during problem formulation:

(1) Reviewers should undertake their literature searches with the broadest possible conceptual definition in mind. They should begin with a few central operations but remain completely open to the possibility that other relevant operations will be discovered in the literature. When operations of questionable relevance are encountered, the reviewer should err on the side of making overly inclusive decisions, at least in the early reviewing stages.

(2) To complement conceptual broadness, reviewers should be exhaustive in their attention to the distinctions in study procedures. The slightest suspicion that a difference in study results is associated with a distinction in study methods should receive some testing by the reviewer, if only in a preliminary analysis.

EXERCISES

1. Identify two integrative research reviews that claim to review the same or similar hypotheses. Which review employs the broader conceptual definition? On what other dimensions concerning problem definition do the two reviews differ? What aspect of problem definition in each review do you find most helpful? (If you cannot find two related reviews, use Bar-Tal & Bar Zohar, 1977, and Findley & Cooper, 1983.)

2. Identify a conceptual variable (e.g., "persistence" or "dogmatism") and list the operational definitions associated with it that are known to you now. Go to the library and find several reports that describe research relevant to your topic. How many new operational definitions did you find? Evaluate these with regard to their correspondence to the conceptual variable.

3. For studies on a topic of interest to you, draw up a preliminary coding sheet. Go to the library and find several reports that describe research relevant to the topic. How must you change the coding sheet to accommodate these studies? What did you leave out? (If you cannot think of a relation, use "gender differences in persistence.")

3

The Data Collection Stage

This chapter focuses on several methods for locating studies relevant to a review topic. Informal, primary, and secondary channels for obtaining research reports are described, along with the biases that may be present in each channel. Background material for using four abstracting services is also presented. This chapter concludes with a discussion of threats to validity encountered during data collection and ways to guard against them.

The major decision an inquirer makes during the data collection stage involves picking the *target population* that will be the referent for the inquiry (Williams, 1978). The target population includes those individuals, groups, or other elements that the inquirer hopes to represent in the study. A precise definition of a target population allows the researcher to list all of its constituent elements. Researchers are rarely required to generate such lists, but because the truth or falsity of so many social science hypotheses depends on the elements of interest, it is important that researchers present clear general definitions. The *accessible population* includes those individuals, groups, or elements the inquirer is able pragmatically to obtain (Bracht & Glass, 1968). In most instances, researchers will not be able to access all of a target population's elements because it would be too costly to do so or because some elements are hard to find.

POPULATION DISTINCTIONS
IN SCIENTIFIC INQUIRY

Similarities between primary research and research review. Both primary research and research review involve specifying target and accessible populations. In addition, both types of inquiry require that the researcher consider how the target and accessible populations may differ from each other. To the extent that the elements in the accessible population are not representative of the target population, the trustworthiness of any claims about the target will be compromised. Because it is easier to alter the target of an investigation than it is to access hard-to-find elements, both primary researchers and research reviewers may find they need to restrict or respecify their target population once an inquiry is complete.

Differences between primary research and research reviews. The most general target population for primary social science research can be characterized roughly as "all human beings." Most subdisciplines, of course, respecify the elements to include less grandiose clusters, like all schizophrenics, all Americans, or all schoolchildren. Topic areas delineate targeted people even more specifically.

Accessible populations in social science research are typically much more restricted than targets. Indeed, in 1946, McNemar (1946) called psychology "the science of the behavior of sophomores" and this characterization remains largely accurate today (e.g., Findley & Cooper, 1981). Most social scientists are aware of the gap between the diversity of people they hope their research encompasses and those people actually accessible to them. In fact, this problem is so pervasive that most research journals do not require repeated attention to the difficulty in every research report.

As noted in the introductory chapter, research reviews involve two targets. First, the reviewer hopes the review will cover "all previous research" on the problem. Reviewers can exert some control over this goal through their choice of information sources. The next several sections of this chapter are devoted to what these sources are and how they are used. Second, the reviewer wants the results of the review to pertain to all the elements of interest in the topic area. The reviewer's influence is constrained at this point by the types of individuals who were sampled by primary researchers. Research reviewing thus involves a peculiar process of sampling samplers. The primary researcher samples individuals and the reviewer retrieves researchers. This process is something akin to cluster sampling (Williams, 1978), with the clusters distinguishing people according to the research projects in which they participated. In reality, reviewers typically are *not* trying to draw representative samples of studies from the literature. Instead, they attempt to retrieve an *entire* population of studies. This formidable goal is rarely achieved, but it is certainly more feasible in a review than in primary research.

METHODS FOR LOCATING STUDIES

This section will present some background on the major channels for locating studies. In addition, an attempt will be made to evaluate the kind of information in each channel by comparing its contents to that of "all relevant work," or to the entire population of material the reviewer would find of interest. Regrettably, there are few empirical data on how the contents of different channels differ from each other or from all relevant work, so the comparisons will be speculative. The problem is complicated, of course, by the fact that the effect of the channel on its contents probably varies from topic to topic.

Informal Channels

The first informal source of information available to reviewers is their own research. The primary research that reviewers have conducted personally often has a strong, and perhaps overweighted, impact on their thinking (see Cooper, 1983). Personal research will differ from all relevant research to the extent that the research outcomes are affected by the researcher's expectations. Individual researchers are also likely to repeat the same operations, causing many operational definitions relevant to a topic area to go unexamined in any particular laboratory.

The second informal source is the "invisible college" (Price, 1966). Invisible colleges, according to Crane (1969), are formed because "scientists working on similar problems are usually aware of each other and in some cases attempt to systematize their contacts by exchanging reprints with one another" (p. 335). Through a sociometric analysis, Crane found that most members of invisible colleges are not directly linked to one another but are linked to a small group of highly influential members. In terms of group communication, invisible colleges are structured like wheels—influential researchers are at the hub and less established researchers are on the rim, with lines of communication running mostly to the hub and less often among peripheral members.

Also, according to Crane (1969), invisible colleges are temporary units that deal with special problems and then vanish when the problem is solved or the focus of the discipline shifts. While estimates vary greatly from study to study, there is no doubt that researchers spend a significant amount of their time in informal exchanges through invisible colleges (Griffith & Mullins, 1972).

The structure of invisible colleges and the influence of prominent and active researchers over the information contained in them hints at the biases in the information transmitted through invisible college links. Relative to all of the research that might be ongoing in a topic area, information from an invisible college is probably more uniformly supportive of the findings of the central researchers than evidence based on more diverse sources. For instance, a fledgling researcher who produces a result somewhat in conflict with the hub of an invisible college network is not likely to find that transmitting the result to the central researcher will mean widespread dissemination throughout the network. Disconfirming findings may lead a researcher to leave the network. Also, because the participants in an invisible college use one another as a reference group, it is likely that the kinds of operations and measurements employed in the members' research will be more homogeneous than those employed by all researchers who might be interested in a given topic.

Other informal communications happen outside of invisible colleges. Students and their professors share ideas and pass on to one another papers and articles they find that are of mutual interest. Sometimes, a formal request soliciting recent work will be made of scholars in a field. Occasionally, readers or reviewers of a researcher's past work will suggest references they think are relevant to the topic that were not cited.

Another source of information, bridging the distinction between formal and informal channels, is that of attendance at professional meetings. A multitude of professional societies, structured both by career concerns and topic interests, exist within the social sciences; many of them hold yearly conventions at which papers are presented. By attending these meetings or requesting reprints of the papers delivered, researchers can discover what others in their topic area are doing and what research has recently been completed but has not yet entered the formal communication domain. In comparison to personal research and invisible colleges, the work found in convention programs is least likely to reveal a restricted sample of results or operations.

All of the informal channels share another important characteristic. Informal communications are more likely than formal ones to contain some inferior studies that have not been scrutinized carefully. Because of methodological flaws, these probably will not appear in more public systems. This is true of convention papers even though they do undergo evaluation, because they are typically selected for presentation on the basis of very short descriptions.

A research reviewer who relies solely on informal channels to collect relevant work would be similar to a survey researcher who decides to sample only his or her friends. Given their obvious biases, it is surprising to find how large a role informal channels play in the research retrieval process.

Primary Channels

Primary publications form the initial link between the reviewer and the formal communication system. There are essentially two methods through which a potential reviewer gains access to primary works. First, reviewers can learn of research done in a topic area through the use of their personal libraries or the journals they regularly follow that are carried by their institutional libraries. The Report of the National Enquiry into Scientific Communication found that the average scholar in the humanities and several social science disciplines scanned approximately seven journals and followed four or five other journals on a regular basis (*Scholarly Communication*, 1979). Most scholars said they spent between 10 and 12 hours per week reading scholarly books and journals and that this reading material came largely from their personal subscriptions.

The number of journals available and the amount of research being conducted probably introduces some serious biases if personal libraries are used as the sole or major source of work for research reviews. As Garvey and Griffith (1971) note, because of the amount of information being generated, individual scholars have lost the ability to keep abreast of all information relevant to their specialties through personal readings and journal subscriptions. This would not be a serious problem *if* the journals read by each researcher constituted a random sample of all journals available. However, researchers tend to operate within networks of journals. These journal networks, according to Xhignesse and Osgood (1967), involve a small number of journals that tend to cite other work available in the same journal and a small group of other outlets that also tend to cite one another. Xhignesse and Osgood found that about 30% of the citations in a given journal were to other work that appeared in the same journal and about 37% of citations were to other journals in the same network.

Given that personal libraries are likely to include journals in the same network, it would not be surprising to find some biases associated with the phenomenon. As with the more informal invisible colleges, we would expect greater homogeneity in both research findings and operations within a given journal network than in all the research available on a topic area. Again, however, the appeal of using the personal library and the journal network as a source of information lies in its ease of accessibility and its credibility to the reference group the reviewer hopes will read the review.

A second retrieval channel that uncovers primary publications is called the ancestry approach. Using this procedure, the reviewer retrieves information by tracking the research cited in already-obtained relevant research. Most reviewers are aware of several studies bearing on their topic before they formally begin the literature search. These studies provide bibliographies that cite earlier related research. The reviewer can examine these citations and judge them for their relevance to the problem. The reference lists of cited articles can also be scrutinized. Through reiteration, reviewers work their way back through a literature until either the important concepts disappear or the studies become so old that the reviewer judges their results to be obsolete.

Searching study bibliographies is also likely to overrepresent work that appears within the reviewer's primary network of journals. Researchers tend to cite other work available through the same outlet or a small group of other outlets. We should therefore expect more homogeneity among references found through reference tracking than would be present in all retrievable studies.

Both means for identifying studies through primary publications—personal libraries and the ancestry approach—share another bias. Obviously, published studies and studies found in their bibliographies are likely to overrepresent published research. However, the criteria for whether or not a study is published are not based solely on the scientific merit of the work. First, published research is probably biased toward statistically significant findings. This bias occurs primarily because of the practices and beliefs of researchers. Greenwald (1975) found that if a research project included a rejection of the null hypothesis the researcher intended to submit the result for publication about 60% of the time. On the other hand, if the study failed to reject the null hypothesis the researcher intended to submit the research for publication only 6% of the time. These intentions are probably based on the researcher's beliefs that nonsignificant findings are less interesting than significant ones and that journal editors are more likely to reject null results.

Also, Nunnally (1960) notes that researchers whose findings conflict with the prevailing beliefs of the day are less likely to submit their results for publication than researchers whose work confirms currently held beliefs. Likewise, journal reviewers appear to look less favorably on studies that conflict with conventional wisdom than studies that support it. Bradley (1981) reports that 76% of university professors answering a mail questionnaire said they had encountered some pressure to conform to the subjective preferences of the reviewers of their work.

Along similar lines, Lane and Dunlap (1978) noted that the significance criterion for publication ensures that the size of differences reported in published works will be larger than the actual differences in the population of interest. As an empirical test of this phenomenon, Smith (1980) found 10 instances of research reviews in which the average size of a relation from published studies could be compared with the average relation in unpublished theses and dissertations. In all 10 instances, the relations in the published articles were larger than those in the theses and dissertations.

Primary publications, then, should not be used as the sole source of information for a research review without convincing justification. The use of personal libraries introduces bias by overrepresenting the paradigms and results that are contained in the reviewer's chosen journal network reference group. This bias will also be contained in the exclusive use of the ancestry or reference-tracking approach. In addition, both techniques will overrepresent published research and therefore introduce the biases associated with the tendency for journals to contain only statistically significant results and the pressure to conform to previous findings.

Secondary Channels

The channels of information called secondary sources should form the backbone of any systematic, comprehensive literature search. This is because secondary sources probably contain the information most closely approximating all publicly available research. These sources have the least restrictive requirements for a study to gain entry into the system.

Bibliographies are nonevaluative listings of books and articles that are relevant to a particular topic area. Often the topic areas are quite broad. Bibliographies are often maintained by single scientists or groups of individuals within a particular area, rather than by a formal organization. For instance, Carl White's *Sources of Information in the Social Sciences* (1986) lists bibliographies on topics such as suicide, psychoanalysis, and experimental aesthetics in psychology. It is also possible to find bibliographies of bibliographies. The

Natural Research Council Research Information Service publishes a bibliography of bibliographies in psychology that lists over 2,000 publications.

The use of bibliographies prepared by others can be a tremendous time-saver for a potential reviewer. The problem, however, is that the bibliographies are likely to be of much greater breadth than the reviewer's interest and they may still contain some of the biases discussed above. Also, it is likely that most bibliographies will need updating for recent research. Even with these precautions, the use of bibliographies generated by others is strongly recommended because the compiler has spent many hours obtaining information and the biases involved in generating the bibliographies may obviate the biases that threaten the personal search of the reviewer.

The government system for publishing its own documents is a self-contained information retrieval system and might therefore be missed entirely by a researcher who does not decide to enter this system. Government documents fall into several categories, of which the most relevant to the present purpose is "research documents for specialists." Most government documents are printed by the U.S. Government Printing Office, which also issues a monthly catalogue that indexes the most recently published works. The novice entering the maze of government documents for the first time will probably find the *Guide to U.S. Government Publications* the best starting point. This work does not describe the documents themselves, but does describe the agencies that publish government documents. In addition to federal government documents, state and local governments have published works that should be available in major research libraries.

Finally, the sources of information most likely to prove fruitful to the potential reviewer are the indexing and abstracting services associated with the social sciences. An indexing or abstracting service will focus on a certain discipline or topic area and define its scope to be an explicit number of primary publication outlets. Each article that appears in the primary outlets will then be referenced in the system.

The limitation of indexing and abstracting services is the long time lag, often three or four years, between when a study is completed and when it appears in the system. Also, each service has certain restrictions on what is allowed to enter the system, based on topical or disciplinary guidelines. For instance, *Psychological Abstracts* will include only psychology-related journals (though certainly an exhaustive accounting of these), whereas the Educational Research Information Center indexes will exhaustively contain education journals. Thus a reviewer interested in an interdisciplinary topic needs to access more than one abstracting system. While secondary publications are least restrictive with regard to the studies within a discipline that will be contained in them, it is likely that more than one secondary source will be required for the literature search to be exhaustive.

ABSTRACTING AND INDEXING SERVICES

Two reasons were given above for why a single abstracting service probably cannot provide an exhaustive bibliography on many topics: (1) abstracting services tend to focus on particular disciplines, but research questions are often interdisciplinary; and (2) it typically takes from one to two years for a published report to appear in the abstracting services. A final limitation on the exhaustiveness of abstracting services derives not from their content but from how they are organized. Even though a service may cover exhaustively the journals that are relevant to a topic, a searcher may not necessarily be able to describe his or her topic in a manner that will ensure uncovering every relevant article, because the searcher must enter the abstracting service by specifying keywords associated with particular pieces of research. If a searcher is unaware of certain indexing terms that are applied to relevant articles, or if the indexers omit terms that the searcher employs, it is likely that the searcher will miss some relevant articles. This problem will become clearer when the particulars of several abstracting services are discussed.

What follows is a brief description of the four abstracting and indexing services most frequently employed in the social and behavioral sciences. In recent years, several full-length treatments of how social scientists can use libraries have appeared (e.g., Borchardt & Francis, 1984; Gover, 1983). Of special interest would be *Library Use: A Handbook for Psychology*, prepared under the auspices of the American Psychological Association (Reed & Baxter, 1983). This text covers in greater depth all of the issues in literature retrieval introduced below.

Psychological Abstracts. The most familiar and frequently used abstracting service in the behavioral sciences is *Psychological Abstracts*. This series covers literally every major journal in the world involved with psychology and related fields. *Psychological Abstracts* publishes monthly nonevaluative summaries of psychology articles along with author and subject indexes. Each monthly volume can include over 2,000 entries from journals and books (dissertations were included up to 1980 and foreign literature up to 1987). The abstracts are typically written by the authors of the articles themselves, but indexing terms are applied by *Psychological Abstracts* employees. An annual index is published, typically in two volumes for subjects and one for authors. Each volume is divided into 16 major classifications, including general psychology; psychometrics; developmental, social, and experimental psychology; physical and psychological disorders; and educational and applied psychology.

The broad classifications give searchers their first opportunity to screen out potentially irrelevant articles. The major screening, however, begins with the searcher's use of the *Psychological Abstracts' Thesaurus of Psychological Index Terms*. The *Thesaurus* is much like a dictionary. It compiles the most recent vocabulary used to define psychological terms of present and past interest. Thus before a searcher can enter the *Psychological Abstracts*, he or she needs to have at least one term known to be used frequently to describe research in the area of interest. The searcher locates this term in the "Relationship" section of the *Thesaurus*. The "Relationship" section displays the term the searcher is aware of and then lists other terms of either a broader or narrower range in the same or related fields that have been used by the indexers to categorize documents. Thus from a single term the searcher can expand the pool of potentially relevant terms into related areas. For instance, the illustrative review examining the relation between personality and interpersonal expectancy communication might have included the searcher going to the "Relationship" section in the *Thesaurus* and looking up the term "locus of control," a personality dimension commonly used in research. Figure 3.1 reproduces the *Thesaurus* entry for "internal-external locus of control."

With an appropriate set of terms in hand, the searcher then goes to the annual subject indexes. The searcher looks up each of the terms suggested by the *Thesaurus*. Under each term, the searcher finds a separate entry for each abstract to which it was assigned. Other terms that were used to index the abstract also appear, along with short phrases describing the content of the article—for example, the age, race, and sex of subjects. At the end of this string of descriptors appears an abstract number, which is used by the searcher to locate the full abstract in the separate monthly issues. Figure 3.1 also contains examples of an entry in the subject index and an abstract.

The abstract itself can be retrieved and this fuller (but still short) description used to judge whether the article is relevant. Finally, if the abstract proves interesting, its listing of the author(s), journal, and date of publication can be used to retrieve the full report.

The Educational Resources Information Center. The Educational Resources Information Center (ERIC) provides a multitude of information services for both practitioners and researchers. The ERIC system collects, screens, organizes, and disseminates any literature associated with educational practices or issues. ERIC maintains 16 clearinghouses throughout the country, each focusing on a different facet of education (e.g., adult education, reading, science education).

The ERIC system also has an associated dictionary called the *Thesaurus of ERIC Descriptors*. As in *Psychological Abstracts*, these descriptors are used to index and enter documents into the ERIC system and to assist users in retrieving documents relevant to their searches. In addition to the *Thesaurus*, ERIC publishes two monthly guides to its contents. The first is called the *Current Index to Journals in Education* (*CIJE*). It presents a monthly listing of the periodical literature covering more than 700 major educational and education-related publications. The second is called *Resources in Education* (*RIE*). It presents the abstracts to recently completed research reports and other documents of educational significance. These are indexed by subject, author, institutional source, and type of publication (e.g., book, convention paper). Most documents stored in *RIE* can be retrieved in their entirety through the system. The full documents

A. Relationship Section Entry for Internal-External Locus of Control in the *Thesaurus of Psychological Terms*

```
                          Internal External Locus of Control
Used For ───────────► UF   Control (Locus of)
                           Locus of Control
Broader Terms ──────► B    Personality Traits
Related Terms ──────►R     External Rewards
                           Extrinsic Motivation
                           Internal Rewards
                           Intrinsic Motivation
```

B. Subject Index Entry (partial) for Internal-External Locus of Control (July-Dec 1981)

```
        Internal External Locus of Control
        academic achievement & sex differences, locus of control & self concept,
          bright achieving & underachieving 4th graders, 2138 ◄──────── Abstract Number
        achievement motivation & locus of control, academic ability & GPA, college
          students, 8916
        age & locus of control & achievement motivation, attributions of teachers'
          motive-thematic goals described in relation to individual vs social norms,
          students, 13635
        age & sex & intelligence & locus of control & interpersonal knowledge & length
          of parental separation, responses to parents' divorce, 5-19 yr olds, 5459...

        ─Other terms associated
        with indexed article
```

C. Abstract Entry for Abstract Number 2138 (July 1981)

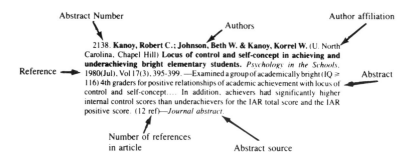

```
        Abstract Number                                      Author affiliation
                                        Authors

        2138. Kanoy, Robert C.; Johnson, Beth W. & Kanoy, Korrel W. (U. North
        Carolina, Chapel Hill) Locus of control and self-concept in achieving and
        underachieving bright elementary students. Psychology in the Schools,
Reference ──► 1980(Jul), Vol 17(3), 395-399. —Examined a group of academically bright (IQ ≥     Abstract
        116) 4th graders for positive relationships of academic achievement with locus of ◄──
        control and self-concept.... In addition, achievers had significantly higher
        internal control scores than underachievers for the IAR total score and the IAR
        positive score. (12 ref)—Journal abstract.

                    Number of references
                    in article              Abstract source
```

Figure 3.1: Examples of Entries in *Psychological Abstracts*

SOURCE: Used by permission of the American Psychological Association.

are typically contained in microfiche collections that can be found in major research libraries.

The steps involved in the use of *RIE* parallel those for the *Psychological Abstracts*. First, the searcher consults the *Thesaurus of ERIC Descriptors*, which is organized like the *Thesaurus of Psychological Terms*. That is, the searcher provides key descriptors relevant to the search and the *Thesaurus* then helps identify broader, narrower, and related terms that might be relevant. Figure 3.2 provides examples of *Thesaurus* and index entries for the term "locus of control." The searcher then consults the monthly issues of *Resources in Education* and the annual indexes for a listing of relevant documents that appear in the volumes associated with each index term. Following these brief article descriptions in the subject index, an accession number appears that can be used to find either the abstract or the full report. The *Current Index of Journals in Education* is entered in the same manner as *Resources in Education*, but the two guides need to be searched separately.

With the accession numbers in hand, the searcher goes to the "Resume" section in either of the guides to find the title, author, source, and abstract associated with the article. In *RIE*, if the article is still deemed potentially relevant the searcher proceeds to the microfiche collection. These contain transparencies that can be placed on microfiche reading machines to bring the document to full size. It is then possible in many libraries to photocopy the magnified microfiche documents to obtain a paper copy of the document. Or the searcher can contact the ERIC Document Reproduction Service to obtain a copy. In *CIJE*, the searcher finds the journal containing the complete document.

Dissertation Abstracts International. While many abstracting services also contain abstracts of dissertations, *Dissertation Abstracts International* (*DAI*) focuses exclusively on this type of document. However, *DAI* is broad in that all dissertations, regardless of discipline, are abstracted in it. Thus the first job of the searcher is to identify those disciplines and subdisciplines that are of interest.

The materials in *DAI* are indexed according to author and important keywords in the dissertation title. No indexer reads each dissertation in order to assign descriptive terms. Instead, a dissertation will appear in *DAI*'s subject indexes only under those important words that appear in the dissertation title. Also, *DAI* volumes contain only the abstracts associated with the dissertations. Most university libraries maintain microfilm copies of only those dissertations completed at that university and therefore, when an abstract appears relevant, the searcher usually must contact the university at which the dissertation was conducted through interlibrary loan to obtain a full-length copy. Alternatively, the searcher can purchase a copy from University Microfilms International in Ann Arbor, Michigan.

Obtaining dissertations is not only time-consuming; it can also be very expensive. If interlibrary loan fails, reviewers might consider writing to dissertation authors and asking to borrow theses or obtain copies of reprints or preprints of articles based on theses. Alternatively, the abstracts of dissertations

A. Alphabetic Descriptor Display Entry for Locus of Control in the *Thesaurus* of ERIC Descriptors

B. Subject Index Entry for Locus of Control in *Resources in Education* (July 1982)

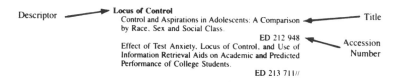

C. Document Resume (partial) for Accession Number ED 213 711 (July 1982)

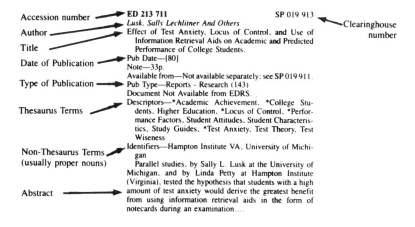

Figure 3.2: Examples of Entries in ERIC

SOURCE: Used by permission of the Educational Resources Information Center.

are generally more detailed than abstracts published in *Psychological Abstracts* or by ERIC. Therefore, it is sometimes possible for a searcher to glean from the abstract itself the information needed to use the dissertation in the research review, if only in a cursory fashion. Figure 3.3 presents some of the features of *DAI*.

The Social Sciences Citation Index. The *Social Sciences Citation Index* (*SSCI*) is unique because it categorizes documents based on the work cited in them as well as their topical focus. According to the publishers of the *SSCI*, "a citation index for the journal literature identifies and groups together all newly published articles that have referenced (cited) the same earlier publication. The earlier publication becomes, in effect, an indexing term for current articles that deal with the same subject" (Institute for Scientific Information, 1980, p. 3). An example will make this strategy clear. At the beginning of a search for locus of control studies, a searcher might be aware of several standard measures of locus of control. One such measure, called the Intellectual Achievement Responsibility (IAR) Scale, was developed by Virginia C. Crandall (Crandall, Katkovsky, & Crandall, 1965). With this knowledge, the searcher could enter the *SSCI* by looking up "Crandall, V. C." in the "Citation Index" volumes, where he or she would find a listing of all articles for which "V. C. Crandall" was the first author that had been cited in other articles during the covered period. Each article that had cited a Crandall work would be listed by its author, source, and date of publication. Those articles citing Crandall et al.'s 1965 publication could have correlated the IAR scale with an interpersonal expectancy measure. A starting point for screening articles on this basis might be the *SSCI* Source Index, which lists publications making citations alphabetically and contains full titles and bibliographical references to the articles as well as summaries of the articles' citations. After using the Source Index, the searcher can go directly to the full report. Figure 3.4 presents an example of a citation index entry.

Citation indexes are most useful when particular researchers or research papers are closely associated with a problem area. The searcher can retrieve studies that cite central researchers in an area and then screen theses for topic relevance. Perhaps the most remarkable thing about the *SSCI* is the breadth of its social science coverage. The *SSCI* indexes every article in over 1,500 journals that cover 50 different social science disciplines, and selectively covers nearly 3,000 other journals that might or might not have social science information in them. Through this process the *SSCI* compiles more than 130,000 new journal articles every year.

The *SSCI* also contains a subject index, called the Permuterm Subject Index, that uses the significant words in article titles to index documents. Every significant title word is paired with every other significant title word, creating a two-level indexing system. Thus a searcher can take a single term and find it in the Permuterm Index and then examine the paired terms that might prove relevant to the relation under study. This feature of the *SSCI* is also illustrated in Figure 3.4.

A. Keyword Title Index Entry for "Locus" (partial) *(Humanities and Social Sciences,* November 1981)

B. Dissertation Abstract (partial) from p. 2033-A *(Humanities and Social Sciences,* November 1981)

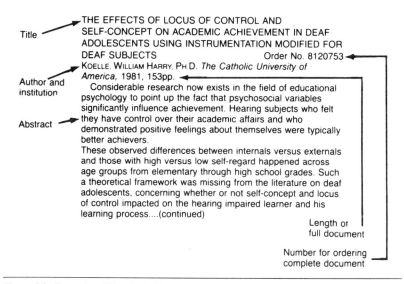

Figure 3.3: Examples of Entries in *Dissertation Abstracts International*

SOURCE: The dissertation titles and abstracts contained here are published with the permission of University Microfilms International, publishers of *Dissertation Abstracts International* (Copyright © 1981 by University Microfilms International), and may not be reproduced without their prior permission.

A. Citation Index Entry (partial) under Crandall, VC (1981, Annual)

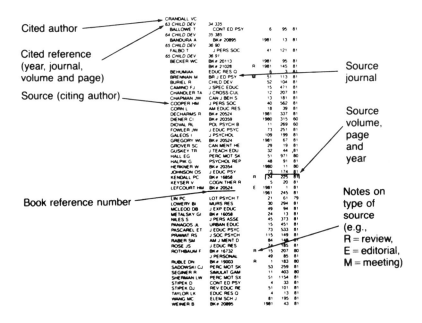

Cited author

Cited reference
(year, journal,
volume and page)

Source (citing author)

Book reference number

Source journal

Source volume, page and year

Notes on type of source (e.g., R = review, E = editorial, M = meeting)

B. Permuterm Index Entry for Locus-of Control (1981, Annual)

Primary term

Co-terms

First author of article

Figure 3.4: Examples of Entries from *Social Sciences Citation Index*

SOURCE: Reprinted with permission of the Institute for Scientific Information® from Social Sciences Citation Index® 1981 Annual. Copyright 1982 by ISI.®

Space limitations make it impossible to examine each of the hundreds of abstracting services available in the social sciences. As of late 1986, there were over 3,000 services available (Katz, 1987), most through the use of on-line computer searches. The content of these services varies from broad coverage of disciplines, as in the ERIC system, to highly specialized topic areas (e.g., alcohol and drug abuse, marriage and the family, exceptional children). Information on abstracting services can be obtained from your librarian or from the *Directory of Online Databases*.

Computer searches. The social science indexing and abstracting services allow the searcher to access thousands of documents from a wide variety of sources. These systems' exhaustiveness, coupled with the explosion in social science research, however, do not solve the problem of information overload so much as underscore it. The reader may have been struck by the time needed to conduct a comprehensive search of any of the four abstracting services, if a topic is broad. Without considerable time and money, it might appear that a thorough search of the abstracts is beyond the capability of a single searcher or even a search team.

Luckily, the computer revolution has touched the scientific communication system and has greatly reduced the effort needed to accomplish an exhaustive literature search. Instead of spending many hours manually searching the abstracting systems, a searcher can use a computer to access several abstracting services in just one or two hours. All major research libraries have on-line computer searches available. The services are also available to private users through telecommunication networks such as CompuServe. These can access the thousands of abstracting services that have been placed on computer tapes. The tapes are accessible through phone hookups to central computer storage facilities. For instance, the DIALOG/Information Retrieval Service has been in use since 1972. The DIALOG system stores more than 200 abstracting services and contains millions of records. Compact discs have also found use in this type of information storage. Universities can purchase subscriptions to discs that are updated periodically. For instance, Silver Platter Information, Inc., makes both *Psychological Abstracts* (called *PsychINFO* in its computer form) and ERIC indexes available on compact discs.

A searcher does not have to know how to operate computers to use the computer search services, though many universities make the hookups available for unsupervised use. Research libraries employ trained specialists who can conduct searches on behalf of searchers once they have the needed information. Typically, the searcher tells the librarian the topic of interest and, most important, what terms, synonyms, and related terms are involved in the search. The librarian and the searcher can browse through the thesauri to identify terms that the searcher might not have considered initially. Searchers are also often asked by the librarian to provide examples of documents they hope to retrieve, to give the librarian some concrete idea about the material desired.

Each of the four abstracting services described above has a slightly different technique for retrieval through the computer. For instance, *PsychINFO* can be accessed using several different computer retrieval techniques. First, the *Thesaurus* can be used to identify a "descriptor field." That is, as noted above, every document included in *PsychINFO* has been read by an indexer and assigned a series of terms (taken from the *Thesaurus*) that describe the document's contents. One can then retrieve documents by asking the computer to identify those that have been assigned the relevant descriptors. It takes the computer only seconds to tell how many documents have been assigned a descriptor and to print out examples of the documents covered.

A second technique is to use "natural language" or "free text" to identify terms that appear in the article title or abstract. The use of natural language descriptors frees the librarian and searcher from relying on the *Thesaurus* and the judgment of the indexer for identifying documents that might be relevant. This technique is especially useful if the searcher is interested in new terms that have not found their way into the *Thesaurus*.

A third method is to use the "identifier field." The identifier field contains, among other significant phrases, the proper nouns that appear in a document. For example, a searcher interested in examining the literature relevant to the Hawthorne effect would not find the term "Hawthorne effect" in the *Thesaurus*. However, because it is a proper noun, the identifier field can be used to search for all documents that mention the Hawthorne effect. The identifier field is also useful when a searcher wants to find research involving a particular test (e.g., the WISC or Strong Vocational Inventory).

Even more impressive, the computer can use Boolean algebra to retrieve abstracts based on the specified relations between sets of descriptions or terms. For example, a searcher might request the computer to identify all abstracts in which the term "homework" appears with the terms "achievement" or "grades" or "attitudes."

Finally, *PsychINFO* can be searched via the computer by using author names, journals, or institutions. For instance, if the searcher is interested in obtaining all of the research conducted at the Center for Research in Social Behavior, this institutional name could be used to locate relevant documents.

PsychINFO is available on computer tape from the present back to 1967. In some instances, the searcher may be interested in older documents, and these would have to be retrieved manually. Interestingly, however, the computerized abstracts are more up to date than the printed volumes available on the library shelves, because the process of abstracting and indexing articles is now done directly onto computer tape, which is then used to generate the printed volumes.

The computerized ERIC system is similar to *PsychINFO* although, of course, it has its own thesaurus. Also, the ERIC descriptor or index terms are divided into major and minor categories. Thus searchers have the option of retrieving only those studies in which the important terms are a major focus in the document or including those documents that treat their interest only tangentially. The other three means of accessing the system—use of free text, identifiers, and names of authors, journals, or institutions—are also available with ERIC. The ERIC data base is computerized back to 1966.

Dissertation Abstracts International has a much less sophisticated means for computerized retrieval. Documents can be located only through the use of free text terms that appear in dissertation titles. It is possible, however, to circumscribe the search somewhat by requesting that the computer access only a broad subject area. For instance, if the searcher is interested in psychological studies examining the Hawthorne effect, "Hawthorne effect" could be used as the keyword and the computer could be requested to retrieve only studies that appeared in the psychology subject category. It is also possible to search *Dissertation Abstracts International* through the use of the dissertation author or the institution granting the degree.

Dissertation abstracts (from *DAI, American Doctoral Dissertations*, and *Comprehensive Dissertation Index*) have been computerized back to the year 1861.

Subject searches of the *Social Science Citation Index* can be accomplished only through the use of free text terms from article titles. Subject searches can be specified to include only a specific type of document, such as journal articles or book reviews. In order to use the citation index component of *SSCI*, the searcher must provide the reference for which the citation history is of interest. A problem with the use of the citation indexes is that numerous errors are contained in the bibliographic information included in journal articles (Boyce & Banning, 1979). Apparently, authors and editors spend little time proofreading references, so it is often necessary for searchers to retrieve general information on a cited author and then sift through it to identify citations that are not listed accurately. Of course, this is a problem for the manual searcher of *SSCI* as well as for the computerized searcher. The *SSCI* has been computerized back to 1972.

The monetary cost of running a computer search is not prohibitive. In fact, approximately 90% of the searches run in my university's research library cost between $10 and $30, with ERIC searches the least expensive and *SSCI* searches the most expensive.

After meeting with the librarian and interacting with the computer, the searcher can request a printed bibliography that includes the authors, references, titles, and abstracts of every potentially relevant article. These bibliographies are sent through the mail by the computer services and usually arrive less than a week after the search. Bibliographies can also be printed on-line, but at greater expense.

It is impossible to overemphasize the value of the computer search to the research reviewer. Using computers, the reviewer can obtain an exhaustive listing of potentially relevant documents with phenomenal speed. Because of the amount of time saved and the convenience of having a hard copy of the search outcome, which can then be evaluated at the reviewer's convenience, the search can be much broader than if it were undertaken manually.

Computer searching is not without problems. In particular, when the computer is used, keywords must be completely specified before the search begins, eliminating the possibility of following up any promising leads that might arise during the search (Menzel, 1966; Stoan, 1982). If computerized searches precluded manual searches, the loss of accidental discoveries would be troubling indeed. However, the searcher is still free to browse, and browsing is recommended before the computer search begins. In browsing, the searcher can expand the keywords to be used in the computer search and identify relevant articles that should appear on the computer printout. Then, if those articles do not appear, he or she will know that something has gone awry. For a more detailed overview of on-line searches and services, see W. A. Katz's *Introduction to Reference Work* (Vol. 2) (1987).

Finally, there is empirical evidence that computer searching has some beneficial by-products. In an experimental study, Feinberg (1981) assigned students to either a "standard bibliographic skills" group or a computer search group for doing term papers. He found students in the computer search group received higher grades, believed the library was more adequate for literature reviews, and derived more satisfaction from the assignment than students who used standard bibliographic procedures.

DETERMINING THE ADEQUACY OF
LITERATURE SEARCHES

The question of which and how many sources of information to use has no general answer. The appropriate sources will be a function partly of the topic under consideration and partly of the resources of the reviewer. As a rule, however, I suggest that searchers should always employ multiple channels so that the chances of a strong unidentified bias distinguishing included from unincluded studies is small. If a reviewer has uncovered different studies through channels that do not share similar biases, then the overall conclusions of the review should be replicable by another reviewer using different, but also complementary, sources for primary research. This rule embodies the scientific criterion of replicability.

Informal sources revisited. Earlier in this chapter, it was noted that the information contained in informal channels is not likely to reflect information gleaned from all potential sources. This research, however, was also shown to complement that gained through formal channels because it is likely to be more recent. Therefore, searchers should not exclude it but should carefully examine the percentage of the total relevant literature that is made up of information retrieved through informal sources. If this percentage is large, the searcher should go to other, secondary, sources before terminating the search.

Published versus unpublished research. It was also mentioned earlier that concentrating only on published research will produce a set of studies that overemphasize significant results. However, it may be counterargued that published research has undergone the most rigorous methodological appraisal by established researchers and probably is of the highest quality.

A focus on only published research might be legitimate in two circumstances. The first is when the published research contains several dozen, or in some cases several hundred, relevant works. In such an instance it is likely that while the published research may overestimate the magnitude of a relation, it probably will not incorrectly identify relation direction. The suggested magnitude of the relation can be cautiously interpreted. Also, enough instances of a hypothesis test will be covered to allow a legitimate examination of which study characteristics covary with study outcomes.

Second, there are many hypotheses that have multiple testings in the literature that were *not* the primary focus of the research. For instance, many psychological and educational studies include gender as a variable in the research design and report hypothesis tests of gender differences, although these are only an ancillary interest of the primary researchers. The bias toward significant results in publications probably does not extend much beyond the primary hypothesis. Therefore, a hypothesis that appears in many articles as a secondary interest of the researcher will be affected by the publication bias to a lesser degree than will the researcher's primary focus.

Generally speaking, however, focusing only on published studies is not advisable. In fact, as we shall see in Chapter 4, publication does not ensure that only studies of high quality will be included in the review. Faulty studies often make their way into print, and well-conducted studies may never be submitted for publication.

In addition, reviewers should not restrict their searches to published outlets even if they ultimately decide to include only published work in their reviews. To make well-informed choices about what to put in and what to leave out of a synthesis, and even to help them decide what the important issues are in a field, reviewers need to have a thorough grasp of the literature.

An empirical examination of search strategies. What searching techniques are actually used by research reviewers? Table 3.1 presents the results of a survey of 57 authors of research reviews published in journals and books covering psychology and education (Cooper, 1987). Authors indicated whether or not they used each of 15 different searching strategies, how useful they found each strategy, and how central or significant the references it yielded were.

On average, reviewers reported using six or seven different strategies. Three of the four most frequently used strategies were associated with the ancestry approach (i.e., examining the references in past reviews, books, and journal articles). Invisible college contacts were also a source of references for many reviewers, though these proved neither as useful nor as central. Some 61% of the reviewers conducted computer searches, and these yielded highly valued references. Searches of citation indexes were not used by many reviewers. However, among those who did use them the resulting references were rated very highly.

The illustrative reviews. To gather the homework literature, several complementary searching strategies were employed. First, four computerized

TABLE 3.1
Use, Utility, and Centrality of Different Sources of References

Use^a	$Utility^b$	Source of References	$Centrality^c$
35	2.6	computer search of abstract data bases (e.g., ERIC, *Psychological Abstracts*)	3.1
32	4.0	manual search of abstract data bases	4.5
5	4.5	computer search of citation index (e.g., *SSCI*)	3.7
8	4.0	manual search of citation index	3.1
53	2.7	references in review papers written by others	2.6
47	3.9	references in books written by others	3.4
40	3.3	references in nonreview papers from journals you subscribe to	3.4
31	4.0	references in nonreview papers you browsed through at the library	4.3
44	4.8	communication with people who typically share information with you	4.3
20	5.4	formal requests of scholars you knew were active in the field (e.g., solicitation letters)	4.5
22	6.1	informal conversations at conferences or with students	5.6
18	5.6	topical bibliographies compiled by others	5.6
15	6.3	browsing through library shelves	5.8
5	7.2	general requests to government agencies	5.2
9	7.3	comments from readers/reviewers of past work	5.5

SOURCE: Cooper (1987).
a. Use is the number of reviewers (out of 57) who said they used the source to locate references.
b. Utility is the average ranking of the source with regard to the number of references it yielded (only by authors who used the source).
c. Centrality is the average ranking of the source with regard to the "significance" or "centrality" of the references it yielded (only by authors who used the source).

research services were accessed: ERIC, *PsychINFO*, the Government Printing Office Monthly Catalog, and the National Technical Information Service. In all cases the natural language or free text keywords used to retrieve documents were "homework" or the word "home" adjacent to the word "work." If these appeared anywhere in the article abstract, the document was retrieved. ERIC included 346 homework citations, and *PsychINFO* included 249. The government services added an additional 48 citations. Obviously, not all of these were research reports.

Additional strategies were employed in order to retrieve studies of homework either too old or too new to be included in the on-line search services. To find older studies (and some missed by the computer because homework was not mentioned in the abstract), the reference lists of past reviews and relevant primary research reports were examined. To find newer studies, letters were sent to 13 researchers who had made recent contributions to the homework literature. Also, 25 requests for information were sent to the deans of education schools ranked as the most productive educational research institutions. The deans were asked to bring the homework review project to the attention of their faculties and to ask that relevant documents be sent. Finally, convention programs from the American Educational Research Association were examined for possible papers and symposia that included presentations on homework.

None of the strategies described so far helps to locate the "fugitive literature," reports that never become a part of the traditional channels of scientific communication. Homework is the kind of topic about which a large amount of fugitive literature might exist. Therefore, letters of inquiry were sent to the 53 state agencies that deal primarily with education, as listed in the *National Directory of State Agencies*. Finally, requests were sent to 110 directors of research and evaluation in selected North American school districts.

The literature search for the review of how research design affects response rates to questionnaires was quite different. *Psychological Abstracts, SSCI, BRS/Inform*, and *Management Contents* were used as parts of the computerized abstract search with the keywords "response rate," "inducement," "incentive," "survey," and "questionnaire." This search, as the descriptors indicate, was one for which the computer was least effective in uncovering relevant research. The reason, of course, was the difficulty in generating a list of descriptors that captured adequately the nature of the hypothesis under study. The computer uncovered 98 citations; of these, 25 were ultimately deemed relevant. Not surprisingly, however, a tracking of the references mentioned in these 25 articles (and past reviews) revealed an additional 68 relevant studies. Thus a total of 93 relevant articles were obtained that included 497 response rates that could be associated with different techniques. The literature search was also restricted to research that had been conducted after 1965. The age-of-research restriction was employed because it was felt that research previous to 1965 might not reflect accurately the response habits of present-day populations.

Without going into detail, the search for studies examining personality moderators of interpersonal expectancy effects on photo-rating tasks revealed 17 research reports that contained at least one relevant comparison. The drug-treatment-of-hyperactivity search found 61 relevant studies.

VALIDITY ISSUES IN STUDY RETRIEVAL

At the beginning of this chapter, it was mentioned that literature searches have two different targets—previous research and individuals or elements relevant to the topic area. It is necessary, therefore, for research reviewers to address the adequacy of their accessed studies with respect to each of the targets. The reviewer must ask (1) how the retrieved studies might differ from all studies and (2) how the elements contained in retrieved studies might differ from all elements of interest. Much of this chapter has dealt with how to answer the first of these questions. Every study does not have an equal chance of being retrieved by the reviewer. It is likely that studies contained in the reviewer's retrieval channels are different from studies that never become public or that can be accessed through other channels. Therefore, the reviewer must pay careful attention to what the inaccessible studies might have to say and how this might differ from what is contained in studies that have been retrieved.

The reviewer's second population of interest, referring to individuals or other basic units of analysis, injects a note of optimism into the discussion. There is some reason to believe that research reviews will pertain more directly to an area's target population than will the separate primary research efforts in the topic area. The overall literature can contain studies conducted at different times, on adults and children, and in different countries with varied racial and ethnic backgrounds (as well as under different testing conditions with different methods). For certain problem areas containing numerous replications, the population of referent individuals accessible to a reviewer may closely approximate the target population of the primary researcher. While a resignation to population restrictions in primary research is understandable, we need not be so acquiescent about the referent population of research reviews. We must bear in mind, of course, that the bias against null and contradictory findings may affect the available samples of elements as well as the sampled studies of the review. To the extent that more retrievable studies are associated with particular subpopulations of elements, the retrieval bias will restrict the accessible populations of individuals.

The first threat to validity associated with the data-gathering phase is that the studies in the review probably will not include all studies pertinent to the topic of interest. Again, reviewers should access as many information channels as needed to ensure that no obvious, avoidable bias exists, within the limits set by cost-effectiveness.

The second threat to validity occurring during study retrieval is that the individuals or elements in the retrieved studies may not represent all individuals or elements in the target population. Of course, the primary researcher's choice of units is beyond the control of the research reviewer, but the reviewer is obligated to describe the missing populations carefully and to qualify any conclusions based on missing or overrepresented samples.

Protecting Validity

(1) The most crucial protection against threats to validity caused by inadequate data collection comes from a broad and exhaustive search of the literature. While the law of diminishing returns does apply here, a complete literature

search has to include at least one major abstracting service, informal communications, and the bibliographies of past research or reviews. The more exhaustive a search, the more confident a reviewer can be that another reviewer using many but perhaps not identical sources of information will reach a similar conclusion.

(2) In their manuscripts, reviewers should be explicit about how studies were gathered, including information on sources, years, and keywords covered in the search. Without this information, the reader of the review has no way of comparing the validity of a particular review's conclusion with the conclusions that may be contained in other reviews.

(3) Reviewers should present whatever indices of potential retrieval bias are available to them. For instance, Rosenthal and Rubin (1982) distinguished published research from dissertations to determine if the evidence from the two sources differed. Cooper, Burger, and Good (1981) reviewed only published studies but speculated that little publication bias was present in their conclusions because the report titles rarely mentioned the hypothesis of interest (i.e., gender differences in locus of control).

(4) The research reviewer should summarize the sample characteristics of individuals used in the separate studies. Given the general gloom that accompanies most discussion of sample representativeness in the social sciences, many reviewers will find this practice reveals an unexpected strength rather than weakness in their research reviews.

EXERCISES

1. Count the number of abstracts indexed under the terms "cognitive dissonance" and "learned helplessness" in the yearly indexes to *Psychological Abstracts* from 1965 to the present. What does this tell you about research in these two areas? What does it tell you about the completeness of *Psychological Abstracts* listings on these two topics?

2. Define a topic area by specifying the keywords (and their crossings or intersections) that would guide a literature search. Pick a few years and do a manual search of an abstract service to locate relevant articles. Perform a parallel computer search. How are the two outcomes different? Which search was more useful and cost-effective?

3. For a topic of your choice, decide what channels you would use to search the literature and the order in which you would access them. For each step in the search, describe its strengths, limits, and cost-effectiveness.

4

The Data Evaluation Stage

This chapter details three approaches to judging methodological adequacy. Also discussed are problems encountered in retrieving data from studies and the procedures used to identify independent hypothesis tests when multiple tests or multiple studies are reported. The chapter concludes with a discussion of validity issues relevant to the data evaluation stage.

The data evaluation stage in a scientific endeavor involves making judgments about whether or not individual data points should be included in the inquiry. This activity must be carried out regardless of whether the data points are the scores of individuals or the outcomes of studies. Data evaluation requires the establishment of criteria for judging the procedural adequacy of how the data were generated. Inquirers must examine all of the potential influences on each data point that may make it irrelevant to the problem under consideration. Then they must determine whether or not these influences are substantial enough to require that the data point be dropped from the inquiry.

EVALUATIVE DECISIONS IN
SCIENTIFIC INQUIRY

Similarities between primary research and research review. Both primary researchers and research reviewers examine their data sets for wild values, errors in recording, or other unreliable measurements. In primary research, individual data points are compared to sample distributions to discover if they are so extreme as to be of questionable validity (that is, statistical outliers; see Barnett & Lewis, 1978). The search for statistical outliers in research reviews involves the examination of relationship magnitudes to determine if the strength of a relation in any study is too different from those in other studies to be considered reliable. Errors in recording are identified in both kinds of research through recalculation of results or the examination of wild values. A primary researcher may observe that a given individual's score is not on the scale of values employed for that particular variable. A research reviewer may recalculate the values of statistical tests presented in a study and find that the primary researcher's calculations were in error.

Differences between primary research and research review. Other means for identifying unreliable data are different for the two types of inquiry. In primary research, an individual's responses are sometimes discarded because surrounding evidence reveals that the individual did not attend to the appropriate stimuli or that the response instructions were misunderstood (see Carlsmith et al., 1976). If deception or some other form of misdirection was used in the research, individual data may be discarded because the participant did not believe the cover story or deduced the hidden hypothesis.

In research review there is only one potential criterion (beyond discordancy and error) for discarding data: the validity of the study's methods. Reviewers decide whether each study was conducted in a careful enough manner so that the result can be trusted. Reviewers can make either a discrete decision (to include the study or not) or a continuous one (to weight studies according to their relative degrees of trustworthiness). A large part of this chapter will be devoted to criteria for judging the methodological quality of a study.

Most social scientists agree that methodological quality should be the primary criterion for decisions about how much trust to place in a study's results. However, in practice the predispositions of reviewers about what the outcome of the review should be often have a strong impact on how studies are evaluated. It is important to examine the sources and effects of reviewers' prior beliefs.

PREDISPOSITIONS OF THE REVIEWER

Almost every primary researcher and research reviewer begins an inquiry with some idea about its outcome. In primary research, methodologists have constructed elaborate systems of controls to eliminate artifactual results created by experimenter expectancy effects (Rosenthal, 1976). In research reviews no such system of controls has been employed. Reviewers are fully aware of their biases *and* the outcomes of studies as the research is being evaluated. This leads to the possibility that the evaluation of research will be colored by its outcomes. The impact of predispositions on reviews has been so great that Gene Glass (1976) made the following remark about the process:

> A common method for integrating several studies with inconsistent findings is to carp on the design or analysis deficiencies of all but a few studies—those remaining frequently being one's own work or that of one's students or friends—and then advance the one or two "acceptable" studies as the truth of the matter. (p. 4)

Mahoney (1977) called this "confirmatory bias," and he performed an experiment that directly tested the impact of predispositions on the evaluation of research. He sampled guest editors for the *Journal of Applied Behavior Analysis* and asked them to rate several aspects of a controlled manuscript. Mahoney found that the methods, discussion, and contribution of the manuscript were evaluated more favorably if the study confirmed the reviewer's predisposition about the results. In a related study, Lord, Ross, and Lepper (1979) found that readers rated proattitudinal studies as better conducted than counterattitudinal studies. More strikingly, the undergraduates who participated in the Lord et al. study showed *polarization* in attitudes despite the fact that they all read the same research abstracts. That is, even though all participants read one study that supported their prior belief and one that refuted it, after reading the two studies participants saw more support for their initial positions.

It appears then that predispositions toward a review's results can influence the reviewer's judgment about the methodological quality of a piece of research. If a study disconfirms the reviewer's predisposition, the reviewer is more likely to attempt to find some aspect of the study that renders it irrelevant or methodologically unsound. On the other hand, studies that confirm the predisposition may be included although their relevance is questionable or their methods flawed.

JUDGING RESEARCH QUALITY

Problems with quality judgments may be even more extensive than those associated with reviewer predispositions. It may be the case that even "disinterested" judges of research could not agree on what is and is not a quality study.

Studies of evaluator agreement about research quality. Several studies have examined the reliability of judgments made about manuscripts submitted to journals in the field of psychology. These studies typically calculate the correlation between the recommendations made by manuscript readers concerning whether or not a manuscript should be accepted for publication. In many respects the judgments of manuscript evaluators are more complex than those of research synthesizers. The manuscript evaluator must consider several dimensions that do not interest the research synthesizer, including the clarity of writing and the interests of the journal's readership. Also, a journal editor will sometimes deliberately choose evaluators who represent different perspectives, while still hoping that the evaluators will agree on the disposition of the manuscript. And, of course, if perfectly objective criteria were available (and were employed), the evaluators would come to concurring decisions.

The interclass correlations reported in studies of manuscript evaluators' agreement on publication decisions range from $r = +.54$ (reported by Scarr & Weber, 1978) to $r = +.19$ (reported by Cicchetti & Eron, 1979). Marsh and Ball (1981) collected judgments on the "quality of research design and analysis" and found the interjudge reliability was $r = +.27$.

In an interesting demonstration, Peters and Ceci (1982) resubmitted 12 already-published research articles to the journals in which they initially appeared. The manuscripts were identical to the originals except that the names and institutions of the submitters were changed from "high status" to "low status." Only 3 of the 12 articles were detected as being resubmissions. Of the 9 articles that completed the re-review process, 8 were *not* accepted for publication. The journal in which the Peters and Ceci (1982) report appears, *The Behavioral and Brain Sciences*, contains open peer commentary on this study and peer review in general.

Some of the differences between judgments by manuscript evaluators and research synthesizers were controlled for in a study conducted by Gottfredson (1978). He removed much of the variability in judges' ratings that might be due to differing initial biases by asking authors to nominate experts competent to evaluate their work. Gottfredson was able to obtain at least two expert evaluations for each of the 121 articles. The experts evaluated the quality of the articles on a three-question scale that left the meaning of the term *quality* ambiguous. An interjudge agreement coefficient of r = +.41 was obtained. On a 36-item evaluation scale that tapped many explicit facets of research quality, an interjudge agreement coefficient of r = +.46 was obtained.

A judgment of the overall quality of a study requires the evaluator to assess and combine several dimensions along which studies can differ. It is therefore possible to locate two sources of variance in evaluators' decisions: (1) the relative importance they assign to different research design characteristics and (2) their judgments about how well a particular study met a design criterion. To demonstrate the first source of variance, I asked six experts in school desegregation research to rank order the importance of six design characteristics for establishing the "utility or information value" of a school desegregation study (Cooper, 1986). The six characteristics were (1) the experimental manipulation (or, in this case, the definition of desegregation), (2) the adequacy of the control group, (3) the validity of the outcome measure, (4) the representativeness of the sample, (5) the representativeness of the environmental conditions surrounding the study, and (6) the appropriateness of the statistical analyses. The intercorrelations of the rankings among the experts varied from r = +.77 to r = +.29, with the average correlation being r = +.47.

In sum, the studies of evaluator agreement are somewhat disheartening. It should be pointed out, however, that the intraclass correlation used to measure agreement has been criticized as being too conservative (Whitehurst, 1984). Also, the reliability of judgments can be enhanced by adding more judges. That is, a decision to accept or reject an article for publication based on ten evaluators' ratings will, on average, correspond more with the consensus of ten other evaluators than with any two evaluators' decisions. Rarely, however, are very large pools of evaluators used to make quality judgments about research by either journal editors or research synthesizers.

A priori exclusion of research versus a posteriori examination of research differences. The studies of agreement about research quality and the role of predispositions in the evaluation process demonstrate instances in which subjectivity intrudes on attempts to reach consensus about our world. The point is important because there is considerable disagreement about whether or not a priori judgments of research quality should be used to exclude studies from research reviews.

This debate was perhaps best captured in an exchange of views between Hans Eysenck (1978) and Gene Glass and Mary Smith (1978) concerning Smith and Glass's (1977) review of research on psychotherapy. Smith and Glass (1977) reviewed over 300 studies of psychotherapy with no a priori exclusion of studies due to poor methodology. Eysenck felt this strategy represented an abandonment of scholarship and critical judgment:

> A mass of reports—good, bad, and indifferent—are fed into the computer in the hope that people will cease caring about the quality of the material on which the conclusions are based. . . . "Garbage in-garbage out" is a well-known axiom of computer specialists; it applies here with equal force. (p. 517)

Eysenck concluded that "only better designed experiments than those in the literature can bring us a better understanding of the points raised" (p. 517).

In rebuttal, Glass and Smith (1978) made several points already mentioned in this chapter and earlier ones. First, as noted in Chapter 2, the poor design characteristics of different studies can "cancel" one another out, if the results of different studies are consistent. Second, the a priori quality judgments required to exclude studies are likely to vary from judge to judge and to be influenced by personal biases. Finally, Glass and Smith claimed they did not advocate the abandonment of quality standards. Instead, they regarded the impact of design quality on study results as "an empirical a posteriori question, not an a priori matter of opinion" (Glass, McGaw, & Smith, 1981, p. 222). They suggested that reviewers thoroughly code the design aspects, good and bad, of each study and then demonstrate if, in fact, the outcomes of studies are related to how the studies were conducted.

The position of Glass and his colleagues seems consistent with a rigorous approach to literature reviewing. The decision to include or exclude studies on an a priori basis requires the reviewer to make an overall judgment of quality that is often too subjective to be credible. Instead, a careful enumeration of study characteristics can be devised by a reviewer and study characteristics can be compared to study results to determine if they covary with one another. If it is empirically demonstrated that studies using "good" methods produce results different from those produced by "bad" studies, the results of the good studies can be believed. When no difference is found it is sensible to retain the "bad" studies because they contain other variations in methods (such as different samples and locations) that, by their inclusion, will help answer many other questions surrounding the problem area.

The only circumstance in which a priori exclusion of studies may be appropriate is when the criteria for excluding studies are defined before the literature is searched, so that the rules do not shift to suit the reviewer, and the number of acceptable studies is large enough to permit the reviewer to substantiate adequately any general conclusions that are drawn. In most cases, however, letting the data speak—that is, including all studies and examining empirically the differences in results associated with methods—substitutes a discovery process for the predispositions of the reviewer.

APPROACHES TO CATEGORIZING RESEARCH METHODS

The decision to take an empirical approach to the impact of research design does not relieve the reviewer of all evaluative responsibilities. The reviewer must still decide what methodological characteristics of studies need to be coded. Obviously, these decisions will depend on the nature of the question under scrutiny and the types of associated research. If a problem has been addressed mainly through experimental manipulations in laboratory settings, a different set of methodological characteristics may be important than if a correlational, field study, or some mix of the two types of research has been used. In the past, research reviewers have employed two approaches to coding methods so that potential differences between "good" and "bad" studies could be assessed. The first approach requires the reviewer to make judgments about the threats to validity that exist in a study. The second approach requires the detailing of the objective design characteristics of a study, as described by the primary researchers.

The Threats-to-Validity Approach

When Campbell and Stanley (1963) introduced the notion of "threats to validity," they literally transformed the social sciences. They suggested that an identifiable set of extraneous influences associated with each research design could be found that "might produce effects confounded with the experimental stimulus" (p. 5). Different research designs had different validity threats associated with them and designs could be compared according to their inferential capabilities. More important, less-than-optimal designs could be "triangulated" so that strong inferences could result from multiple studies when the single, "perfect" study could not be performed.

Campbell and Stanley's notion held the promise of increased sensitivity and objectivity in discussions of research quality. However, it was not long before some problems in the application of their scheme became apparent. The problems related to creating an exhaustive list of threats to validity and identifying what the implication of each threat might be.

Initially, Campbell and Stanley (1963) proposed two broad classes of validity threats. Threats to *internal* validity related to the direct correspondence between the experimental treatment and the experimental effect. To the extent that this correspondence was compromised by deficiencies in research design, the interpretability of a study's results would be called into question. Campbell and Stanley listed eight threats to internal validity. Threats to *external* validity related to the generalizability of research results. Evaluating external validity required assessing the representatives of a study's participants, settings, treatments, and measurement variables. While the external validity of a study could never be assessed definitively, Campbell and Stanley suggested four classes of threats to representativeness.

Next, Bracht and Glass (1968) offered an expanded list of threats to external validity. They felt that "external validity was not treated as comprehensively as internal validity in the Campbell-Stanley chapter" (p. 437). To rectify this omission, Bracht and Glass identified two broad classes of external validity: *population* validity, referring to generalization of persons not included in a study, and *ecological* validity, referring to nonsampled settings. Two specific threats to population validity were described, along with ten threats to ecological validity.

Later, Campbell (1969) added a ninth threat to internal validity, called "instability," defined as "unreliability of measures, fluctuations in sampling persons or components, autonomous instability of repeated or equivalent measures" (p. 411).

Finally, Cook and Campbell (1979) offered a list of 33 specific threats to validity grouped into four broad classifications. The notions of construct validity and statistical conclusion validity were added to internal and external validity. *Construct* validity referred to "the possibility that the operations which are meant to represent a particular cause or effect construct can be construed in terms of more than one construct" (p. 59). *Statistical conclusion* validity referred to the power and appropriateness of the data analysis technique.

From this brief history, the problems in using the threats-to-validity approach to assess the quality of empirical studies should be clear. First, different researchers may use different lists of threats. For instance, should the threat of "instability" offered by Campbell (1969) constitute one threat, as originally proposed, or three threats, as redefined by Cook and Campbell (1979)? Or should ecological validity constitute one threat or up to ten different threats? A second problem is the relative weighting of threats—is the threat involving historical confounds weighted equally with the threat involving restricted generalizability across constructs? Expert methodologists may even disagree on how a particular threat should be classified. For instance, Bracht and Glass (1968) listed "experimenter expectancy effects" as a threat to external validity, while Cook and Campbell (1979) listed it as a threat to the construct validity of causes.

All these problems aside, the threats-to-validity approach to the evaluation of research still represents an improvement in rigor, and is certainly preferable to the a priori single judgment of quality it replaces. Each successive list of threats represents an increase in precision and accumulation of knowledge. Also, the list of validity threats gives the reviewer an explicit set of criteria to apply or modify. In that sense, reviewers who use the threats-to-validity approach make their rules of judgment open to criticism and debate. This is a crucial step in making the research evaluation process more objective.

The Methods-Description Approach

In the second approach to study evaluation, the reviewer codes exhaustively the objective characteristics of each study's methods, as they are described by the primary researchers. This approach was discussed earlier in connection with the study coding sheet (see Chapter 2). Now a more detailed examination is in order.

In Campbell and Stanley's (1963) original work, three preexperimental designs, three true experimental designs, and ten quasi-experimental designs were examined. The list of designs was expanded by Cook and Campbell (1979). In most areas of research considerably fewer than all the available designs will be needed to describe exhaustively how independent and dependent variables have been paired in the relevant research.

As Campbell and Stanley (1963) noted, experimental designs relate mainly to eliminating threats to internal validity. They hold little information about the three other classes of threats to trustworthiness. Some of these were alluded to in Chapter 2, but a bit more detail should be added here. Examining the credibility of, say, experimental manipulations and measurements requires a description of the procedures that the primary researchers used to create independent variables and measure dependent variables. With regard to manipulated independent variables, reviewers can code the number and type of empirical realizations used: In how many ways was the independent variable manipulated? Was the manipulation accomplished through written instructions, films, or the creation of a live-action situation? Similarly, reviewers can record the presence or absence of controls to keep the experimenter blind to the treatment conditions and whether or not deception or misdirection was used to lead the participant away from guessing the hypothesis. Obviously, these considerations are relevant only when treatment manipulations were employed in the studies of interest.

Distinctions in measurement techniques can be codified by recording the number of measures used; whether they were verbal, written, behavioral, or interpersonal judgments; whether they were standardized, informal, or constructed for the particular study; and their relative reliability, if such assessments are available. Other measurement characteristics might be of interest to particular research areas.

As to the population and ecological generalizability of results, it has been suggested that the reviewer can record any restrictions on the types of individuals sampled in the primary studies, when and where the studies were conducted, and when the dependent variable measurements were taken in relation to the manipulation or measurement of the independent variables.

Finally, to assess a study's statistical power, reviewers should record the number of participants, whether a between- or within-subjects design was employed, the number of other factors (sources of variance) extracted by the analyses, and the statistical test used.

One problem with the methods-description approach to evaluating studies is shared with the threats-to-validity approach—different reviewers may choose to list different methodological characteristics. However, the methods-description approach has several advantages. First, when studies are being coded the methods-description approach does not require as much integration of material or inferential judgment. Making a judgment about the threat to validity called "low statistical power" provides a good example. The coder can judge whether a study has a good chance to reject a false null hypothesis only through a combination of several explicit study characteristics: size of the sample, between- or within-subjects design, inherent power of the statistical test (e.g., parametric versus nonparametric), and/or number of other sources of variance extracted in the analysis. Two coders of the same study might disagree on whether or not a study is low in power, but agree perfectly on a coding of the separate components that make up the decision. The objective design characteristics of studies can be coded with less ambiguity of meaning and, therefore, greater reliability. The question then becomes: Is the integration of methodological information when studies are first coded necessary to assess the presence or absence of a validity threat? For a majority of threats, the answer is no. If an analysis of study results shows that, say, only studies using within-subjects designs found significant results, then the reviewer can examine this design feature for all of its implications for validity. That is, between-subjects designs may have been too low in power to reveal an effect, or the premeasure in the within-subjects designs may have sensitized the participants to the independent variable manipulation. Thus, while it may be difficult to retrieve the particular aspect of a research design that created a threat to validity, the reviewer often can still examine validity threats when methodological distinctions are coded.

A Mixed-Criteria Approach

The optimal strategy for categorizing studies appears to be a mix of the two a posteriori approaches. First, the reviewer should code all potentially relevant, objective aspects of research design. However, there are threats to validity that may not be captured by this information alone. For instance, the threats to internal validity involving how a control group is treated—diffusion of treatments, compensatory rivalry, or resentful demoralization in the less desirable treatment—are probably best coded directly as threats to validity, though deciding whether they are present or absent still relies heavily on the description of the study presented by the primary researcher. While this mixed-criteria approach does not remove all problems from study evaluation, it is another step toward explicit objective decision making in an area previously rife with subjective and arbitrary judgments.

The illustrative reviews. Two of the four illustrative reviews provide good examples of how research evaluations can be conducted.

First, the review of the effects of homework included three codings related to the internal validity of studies: the type of experimental design (e.g., random assignment or nonequivalent control groups), whether or not treatments were counterbalanced, and whether or not the experimenter was also the teacher of the classes receiving the treatments. Other codings of the homework studies related to the measurement, external, and statistical validity of studies (see Table 2.1).

Note that the coders of homework studies made no inferences whatever about methods or their validity—they simply gathered information exactly as reported by the primary researchers. Studies that used random assignment, counterbalanced treatments, and nonexperimenter teachers were clearly preferable. However, studies that fell short of this ideal were also included in the review and the impact of the design factors on the actual outcomes of studies was examined. Only if important relations were found between design and outcome were the differences in study results weighted in regard to their relative trustworthiness.

In the review of drug treatments of hyperactivity the selection of studies was restricted to include only those that employed random assignment and double-bind procedures, the strongest possible design for causal inferences. Thus this review did exclude studies on an a priori basis. What was the rationale? A total of 61 studies were found that met very strict methodological requirements—a majority of all the studies identified as potentially relevant. This was a large enough pool of experiments to allow effective examination of the impact of other procedures on study results. That is, other aspects of studies related to other forms of validity varied considerably even within this restricted sample. It will be rare for this type of situation to prevail in the social sciences. When it does, the reviewer may be able to argue convincingly for a priori exclusion of studies. Certainly it would be difficult for a critic of the hyperactivity review to argue that the exclusion of studies was biased by the reviewers' predispositions.

PROBLEMS IN DATA RETRIEVAL

Thus far procedures have been discussed that allow reviewers to find and evaluate research in an exhaustive and rigorous fashion. Some deficiencies in both retrieval and evaluation procedures have been noted that will frustrate reviewers regardless of how thorough and careful they try to be. Some potentially relevant studies do not become public and defy the grasp of even the most conscientious search procedures. With regard to evaluating studies, it is impossible to remove subjectivity from the process completely. A third problem area spans both the retrieval and evaluation phases of literature reviewing. These problems, almost completely beyond the control of the reviewer, involve (1) the inability of libraries to ensure that all documents of potential relevance to the reviewer are on hand, (2) the careless or incomplete reporting of data by primary researchers, and (3) the less-than-perfect information-processing skills of the people who retrieve information from studies. Each of these three problems will be dealt with separately.

Problems in Library Retrieval

Every research reviewer will find that some articles of potential relevance (based on titles or abstracts) cannot be located in his or her personal or institutional library. To what lengths should the reviewer go to retrieve these articles? The use of interlibrary loans is a viable route for attempting to retrieve these studies. As noted earlier, interlibrary loan can even be used to obtain dissertations and master's theses, or dissertations can be purchased from University Microfilms International in Ann Arbor, Michigan. Contacting primary researchers directly is another possibility, although personal contact often results in only a low rate of response. Whether or not a primary researcher can be located and induced to send a reprint is influenced in part by the age of the article requested.

In general, when deciding how to retrieve articles that are difficult to obtain the searcher should consider (1) the percentage of the total of known articles that are difficult to find, (2) the cost involved in undertaking extraordinary retrieval procedures (e.g., interlibrary loan is cheap, buying dissertations is expensive), and (3) any time constraints under which he or she is operating.

Incomplete and Erroneous Results Sections

Perhaps the most frustrating occurrence in study retrieval is when the reviewer obtains a primary research report but the report is incomplete in its description of the results. For instance, in my review of research on gender differences in conformity, I found that 12 of 38 relevant research reports contained no description of the statistics that led to the conclusion (Cooper, 1979). Statistical data were most often omitted from a report when the results of the tests were nonsignificant. Most remarkable was the discovery of four studies that did report statistical data but neglected to mention the direction of the relation!

Obviously, incomplete reporting of statistical values will be of primary concern to research reviewers who intend to perform quantitative synthesis (discussed in the next chapter). What should the quantitative reviewer do about missing data? Several conventions can be suggested to handle the most common problems.

First, the reviewer can treat all studies that report hypothesis tests as "non-significant" without reporting the associated inference test value, p-levels, or effects sizes as having uncovered exactly null results. That is, for any statistical analysis involving these studies, a probability of .5 (in the one-tailed instance) and a relationship strength of zero is assumed. It is reasonable to expect that this convention has a conservative impact on any quantitative review results. In general, when this convention is used, cumulative p-levels should be higher and the average relationship strength closer to zero than if the exact results of these studies were known.

Another convention involves attempting to combine results when some primary researchers use parametric statistics and others use nonparametric statistics. In most cases one statistical paradigm will predominate greatly over the other across the entire set of studies. In this instance the different statistics can be aggregated as though they all shared the dominant set of assumptions without greatly distorting the results. If the split between parametric and nonparametric tests is roughly even, the two sets of studies should be examined separately.

Reviewers who want to perform statistical combinations sometimes find that separate studies are incommensurable because they employ different numbers of factors in their analysis. For instance, one study on drug treatments of hyperactive children might present a simple t-test comparison of a treated and control group. Another study might have employed the gender and age of children as additional factors in an analysis of variance design. All else being equal—and assuming some gender and age effects—the second experiment will produce a lower probability level and a larger treatment effect because the amount of error against which the treatment-control difference is compared will be smaller. Glass et al. (1981) have outlined procedures for equating statistical results from studies using different numbers of factors in their analytic design, but in practice primary researchers rarely report their results in enough detail for a reviewer to carry out the needed transformations. When this is the case, the reviewer should determine empirically whether the statistical results of a study are related to the number of factors in the analysis. If a relation is found, the reviewer should report separately the results obtained from analyses of studies that used only the single factor of interest.

In addition to incomplete reports, some reports are inexact in their statistical data. Many reports will describe statistical tests as reaching the $p < .05$ level of significance rather than describing the exact probability associated with the outcome of the inference test. In this case the reviewer can recalculate the p-levels to reflect their exact value.

Finally, there is the problem of errors in statistical analyses. As an empirical demonstration, Wolins (1962) contacted 37 psychologists who had recently published research reports and asked if he could see their raw data. Of these, 26 authors, or 70%, did not reply or claimed their data had been lost or inadvertently destroyed. Of 7 data sets Wolins was able to reanalyze, 3 were found to have large analytic errors.

While no one knows exactly how common errors are in statistical analyses, studies indicate they may be frequent enough to concern research reviewers. Whenever possible, the reviewer should cross-check the statistics presented in research reports to ensure that none of the results implies wild values and all of the results reported about a study are consistent with one another.

Unreliability in Coding Study Results

Just as researchers sometimes make errors in their data analysis, it is also the case that errors are made in the recording of data. Transcription errors are a problem for research reviewers when they extract information from research reports. Rosenthal (1978a) reviewed 21 studies that examined the frequency and distribution of recording errors. These studies uncovered error rates ranging from 0 to 4.2% of all the data recorded; 64% of the errors in recording were in a direction that tended to confirm the study's initial hypothesis.

Stock et al. (1982) empirically examined the number of unreliable codings made in a literature review. They had three coders (one statistician and two post-Ph.D. educational researchers) record data from 30 documents into 27 different coding categories. Stock et al. found that some variables, such as the means and standard deviations of the ages of participants, were coded with perfect or near perfect agreement. Only one judgment, concerning the type of sampling procedure employed by the researchers, did not reach an average coder agreement of 80%.

In sum, while coders of primary research are fairly reliable in their retrieval of information, it is good practice to monitor coder accuracy. This is especially true if the number of studies to be coded is large or if persons with limited research training are called upon to do the coding. In these instances the reviewer should treat the coding of studies as if it were a standard exercise in data gathering. Specifically, coding sheets should be accompanied by codebooks explaining the meaning of each entry. Prior to actual coding, discussions and practice examples should be worked on with coders. Assessments of reliability should be taken on controlled sets of studies. Coding should not begin until an acceptable level of intercoder reliability has been established.

The illustrative reviews. In the review of the effects of homework, fewer than a dozen potentially relevant manuscripts were identified in the literature search that could not be retrieved for examination. Most of these were very old, were published outside North America, or were unpublished. These documents represented less than 5% of all the documents actually judged potentially relevant.

The review of personality moderators of interpersonal expectancy effects had the most difficulty with missing data. This occurred because correlation coefficients were often reported as nonsignificant and the magnitude of the correlation was not given. One technique that helped fill in these missing data was to determine if a published journal article was a report of a dissertation. If it was, the full dissertation was obtained; this often contained more complete descriptions of data outcomes.

Finally, the homework review included a formal test of the reliability with which studies were coded. Kappa coefficients and percentages of agreement were calculated between two coders on thirteen categories. The reliability estimates indicated perfect agreement on seven of the categories. The poorest reliability, $k = .71$ and 79% agreement, occurred on the coders' retrieval of the number of assignments students did each week. Whenever disagreements occurred, the two coders examined the study together and resolved the difference.

IDENTIFYING INDEPENDENT HYPOTHESIS TESTS

Another important decision that must be made during the data evaluation stage involves how to identify independent hypothesis tests. Sometimes a single study may contain multiple tests of the same hypothesis. This can happen for two reasons. First, more than one measure of the same construct might be employed and each measure analyzed separately. For example, a hyperactivity researcher might measure school behavior problems through both teacher reports and classroom observation. Second, different samples of people might be used in the same study and their data analyzed separately. This would occur, for instance, if the hyperactivity researcher examined results for boys and girls separately. In both of these instances, the hypothesis tests are not completely independent—they share historical and situational influences, and in the former case they even share influences contributed by having been collected on the same subjects.

The problem of nonindependence of hypothesis tests can be taken further. Sometimes a single research report can describe more than one study. Sometimes multiple research reports describe studies conducted at the same laboratory. A reviewer might conclude that studies conducted at the same site, even if they appear in separate reports over a number of years, still contain certain constancies that imply the results are not completely independent. The same primary researcher with the same predispositions may be using the same laboratory rooms while drawing participants from the same population.

Especially in instances where the reviewer intends to perform a quantitative synthesis, a decision must be made about when hypothesis tests will be considered independent events. Several strategies can be suggested regarding how to decide on the unit of analysis in research reviews.

Laboratories as Units

The most conservative way to identify independent hypothesis tests employs the laboratory or researcher as the smallest unit of analysis. Advocates of this most conservative approach would suggest that the information value of repeated studies in the same laboratory is not as great as an equal number of studies reported from separate laboratories. (An intraclass r can be computed to assess the empirical degree of independence of studies from the same laboratory.) This approach requires the reviewer to gather all studies done at the same research laboratory and to come to some overall conclusion concerning the results at that particular site. One drawback, therefore, is that it requires the reviewer to conduct reviews within reviews, since decisions about how to synthesize results first must be made within laboratories and then again between laboratories.

This approach is rarely used in practice. It is generally considered too conservative and too wasteful of information obtained by examining the variations in results from study to study.

Studies as Units

Using the study as the unit of analysis requires the reviewer to make an overall decision about the results of comparisons reported in separate studies but not to aggregate results over more than one report.

If a single research report contains information on more than one test of the same hypothesis, the reviewer weights each discrete finding by the number of hypothesis tests in the report or study. This might be done by using the average or median result to represent the study. This procedure ensures that each study contributes equally to the overall review result. For example, a study of homework with two grade levels of students reporting results on five different measures of achievement (e.g., ten hypothesis tests) might be weighted so that a single result comes from the report and this result is given consideration equal to a report with one grade level and one measure.

Obviously, there will be some subjectivity in the reviewer's judgment of what constitutes a study. For instance, one reviewer might consider all results in a single journal article or manuscript as one study. Another reviewer might consider a report that divides results into separate studies as containing more than one study. Regrettably, the delineation is not as clear as we might like it to be.

Samples as Units

This approach permits a single study to contribute more than one hypothesis test, if the hypothesis tests are carried out on separate samples of people. Thus a hyperactivity reviewer would consider hypothesis tests on boys and girls within the same study as independent, but not tests that used alternate measures of the same construct given to the same children. The use of samples as units assumes that most of the variance shared by hypothesis tests in the same study comes from being collected on the same subjects.

Hypothesis Tests as Units

The least conservative approach to identifying comparisons is to use the individual hypothesis test or comparison as the unit of analysis. Each separate test of the hypothesis conducted by primary researchers is regarded as an independent test by the research reviewer. This technique's strength is that it does not lose any of the within-study information regarding potential moderators of the relation. Its weakness is that the assumption that hypothesis tests are independent, needed for most quantitative syntheses of results, will be violated. Also, the results of studies will not be weighted equally in any overall conclusion about results. Instead, studies will contribute to the overall finding in relation to the number of statistical tests contained in it. This is not necessarily a good weighting criterion.

Shifting Units

A compromise approach to identifying comparisons is to employ a shifting unit of analysis. Specifically, each statistical test is initially coded as if it were an independent event. Thus a single study that contained twelve statistical tests or comparisons would have twelve separate coding sheets filled out for it. Each coding sheet would be slightly different, depending on the aspects of the samples, measurements, or design characteristics used to distinguish the statistical test. However, when an overall cumulative result for the review is generated, statistical tests are weighted so that each *study* (all other weighting factors being equal) contributes equally to the general finding. Thus a study containing three correlations would have these averaged and then added as a single number into the analysis across all studies. However, when examining potential moderators of the overall relation, a study's results are aggregated only *within* the separate categories of the influencing variable. For example, if a homework and achievement study presented correlations for males and females separately, this study would contribute only one correlation to the overall analysis—the average of the male and female studies—but two correlations to the analysis of the impact of gender on the relation—one for the female group and one for the male group. To take the process one step further, if this study reported different correlations for class grades and standardized tests within each gender (i.e., four correlations in all), the two correlations for different measurements would be averaged within each gender group when the analysis for gender influence was conducted and the two gender group correlations would be averaged when the measurement moderator was examined. This means that for moderating hypotheses a single study can contribute one test to each of the categories distinguished by the third variable. This strategy is a compromise that allows studies to retain their maximum information value while keeping to a minimum any violation of the assumption of independence of hypothesis tests.

Statistical Adjustment

Raudenbush, Becker, and Kalain (1988) have proposed a statistical solution to the problem of nonindependent hypothesis tests. They have devised a procedure based on generalized least squares regression that statistically adjusts for interdependence among multiple outcomes within studies and for different numbers of outcomes across studies. The key to using their technique successfully lies in the reviewer having credible numerical estimates of the interdependence of hypothesis tests. For instance, assume a study of homework's effects includes both class grades and standard test scores as measures of achievement. In order to use the Raudenbush et al. technique, the reviewer must estimate the correlation between grades and achievement for the sample in this study. Data of this sort often are not provided by primary researchers. They might be estimated from other studies, however, or the analysis could be run with low and high estimates to generate a range of values.

The illustrative reviews. Three of the four illustrative research reviews employed the shifting unit of analysis procedure described above. The only exception was the review of research design effects on response rates to questionnaires. In this analysis, because the raw data from each study could be retrieved and aggregated, only the number of participants in a study determined its weighting. In instances where raw data can be retrieved, they should be used rather than sample statistics (see Chapter 5 for details).

VALIDITY ISSUES IN EVALUATING RESEARCH

The use of any evaluative criteria other than methodological quality introduces a potential threat to the validity of the review outcome. As Mahoney (1977) states, "To the extent that researchers display [confirmatory] bias our adequate understanding of the processes and parameters of human adaptation may be seriously jeopardized" (p. 162). It is safe to assume that evaluative bias has pernicious effects on our understanding.

A second threat to validity occurring during data evaluation involves the unreliability of data introduced by the incomplete reporting of primary researchers. We have seen that many research reports completely omit discussions of hypothesis tests or give only incomplete information on the tests that were mentioned. The greater the percentage of such incomplete reports within a research review, the wider are the confidence intervals that must be placed around the review's conclusion.

Finally, a third threat to the validity of a review involves the unreliability in coding of research results. In most instances coding can be done with fairly high reliability, especially if the strategy employed asks coders only to retrieve information directly as presented by the primary researchers, rather than to make inferences about research quality or the presence or absence of particular validity threats.

Protecting validity. In the course of this chapter several procedures have been described that are designed to increase the objectivity of research evaluation and related decisions:

(1) Reviewers should make every effort to ensure that *only* conceptual judgments influence the decision to include or exclude studies from a review.

(2) If studies are to be weighted differently, the weighting scheme should be explicit and justifiable. Personal involvement in a study is not a legitimate criterion for giving it added weight.

(3) The approach used to categorize study methods should exhaust as many design moderators as possible. The reviewer should detail each design distinction that was related to study results and tell the outcome of the analysis.

(4) More than one study coder should be employed, and intercoder agreement should be quantified and reported. Also, coding sheets should be filled out by coders who are blind to the results of the study.

(5) The reviewer should state explicitly what conventions were used when incomplete or erroneous research reports were encountered.

EXERCISES

1. List a set of criteria that you think distinguish good and bad research. Rank order the criteria with regard to their impact on research quality. Compare your criteria and rankings with those of a classmate. What is similar and different about your lists?

2. With your classmate, agree on a set of criteria and evaluative scales. Also, identify a set of ten studies on the same topic. Independently apply the criteria to the ten articles. Compare your ratings. How did they differ and what led to the differences? How might the criteria be revised to minimize differences in future use?

3. Using the same set of studies, and again in conjunction with a classmate, record the following information from each report: (a) sample size, (b) any restrictions on who was sampled, (c) the means of comparison groups (or other data) on the primary variable of interest, (d) whether or not the hypothesis was confirmed, and (e) the type and significance level of the inference test of primary interest. How many values did you agree and disagree on? Which values led to the most disagreement? Why?

5

The Analysis and Interpretation Stage

This chapter presents some statistical methods that can help reviewers summarize research results. Among the techniques discussed are those that generate cumulative probabilities, those that involve the calculation of an effect size, and those that help the reviewer examine the variability of effect sizes across studies. Finally, validity issues arising during data analysis and interpretation are outlined.

Data analysis and interpretation involve the synthesis of the separate data points collected by the inquirer into a unified statement about the research problem. According to Kerlinger (1973):

> *Analysis* means the categorization, ordering, manipulating and summarizing of data to obtain answers to research questions. The purpose of analysis is to reduce data to intelligible and interpretable form. . . . *Interpretation* takes the results of analysis, makes inferences pertinent to the research relations studied, and draws conclusions about these relations. (p. 134)

As noted in Chapter 1, data interpretation requires that decision rules be used to distinguish systematic data patterns from "noise" or chance fluctuation. Although different decision rules can be used, the rules typically involve assumptions about what noise looks like in the target populations (e.g., normally distributed errors).

INTEGRATING TECHNIQUES IN
THE TWO TYPES OF INQUIRY

Just as any scientific inquiry requires the leap from concrete operations to abstract concepts, both primary researchers and research reviewers must leap from samples of data to more general conclusions. Until the mid-1970s, however, there had been almost no similarity in the analysis and interpretation techniques used by primary researchers and reviewers. Primary researchers were obligated to present sample statistics and to substantiate any assertions about hypotheses with probability tests. Most frequently, primary researchers computed means and standard deviations descriptive of their samples, made the assumptions needed for statistical tests (e.g., normal distribution and independence of errors, homogeneity of variance), and reported the probabilities associated with whether potential sources of systematic variance could be distinguished from error.

Statistical aids to primary data interpretation have not gone uncriticized. Some have argued that significance tests are not very informative because they tell only whether or not the null hypothesis is true (e.g., Oakes, 1986). According to this argument, in a population of people the null hypothesis is almost never true and therefore the significance of a given test is mainly influenced by how many participants have been included in the study. Also, those skeptical about the value of significance test statistics point to limitations in the population of events referred to under parametric assumptions. No matter how statistically significant a relation may be, the results of a study are generalizable only to people like those who participated in that particular research effort.

Skepticism about the value of statistics helps those who use statistics to refine their skills and keep their output in proper perspective. Nonetheless, most primary researchers use statistics in their work and most would feel extremely uncomfortable about synthesizing data without some assistance (or credibility) supplied by statistical procedures.

In contrast to primary researchers, research reviewers were not obligated to apply any standard analysis and interpretation techniques in the synthesis process. Traditionally, reviewers interpreted data using rules of inference unknown even to them. Therefore, a description of the common rules of inference used in research reviews was not possible. Analysis and interpretation methods were idiosyncratic to the particular perspective of the individual reviewer. This subjectivity in analysis and interpretation led to skepticism about the conclusions of many reviews. To address the problem, critics introduced quantitative methods into the reviewing process. These methods build on the primary research statistics contained in the individual studies.

QUANTITATIVE SYNTHESIS OR META-ANALYSIS

It was suggested above that the two recent events that have had the strongest impact on research reviewing are the growth in research and the advent of the computerized literature search. A third strong impact was the introduction of quantitative procedures, called meta-analysis, into the reviewing process.

The explosion in social science research has focused considerable attention on the lack of standardization in how reviewers arrive at general conclusions from series of related studies. For some topic areas a separate verbal description of each relevant study will now be impossible. One traditional strategy, to focus on one or two studies chosen from dozens or hundreds, fails to portray accurately the accumulated state of knowledge. Most certainly, in areas where hundreds of studies exist, reviewers must describe "prototype" studies so that readers understand the methods primary researchers have used. However, relying on the *results* of prototype studies as representative of all studies may be seriously misleading. As we have seen, this type of selective attention is open to confirmatory bias: A particular reviewer may highlight only studies that support his or her initial position. Also, selective attention to evidence cannot give a good estimate of the strength of a relation. As evidence on a topic accumulates, researchers become more interested in the strength rather than the simple existence of a relation. Finally, selective attention to only a portion of all studies places little or imprecise weight on the volume of available testings. Presenting one or two studies without a cumulative analysis of the entire set of results gives the reader no estimate of the confidence that should be placed in a conclusion.

Reviewers also face problems when they consider the variations among the results of different studies. Reviewers will find distributions of results for studies sharing a particular procedural characteristic but varying on many other characteristics. They may not be able to conclude accurately whether a procedural variation affects study results because of the variability in results obtained by any single method or the likelihood that the distributions of results with different methods will overlap. It seems, then, that there are many situations in which reviewers must turn to quantitative reviewing techniques. Gene Glass (1977) has written, "The accumulated findings of . . . studies should be regarded as complex data points, no more comprehensible without statistical analysis than hundreds of data points in a single study" (p. 352).

The application of quantitative inference procedures to reviewing seems to be a necessary response to the expanding literature. If statistics are applied appropriately, they should enhance the validity of review conclusions. Quantitative reviewing is an extension of the same rules of inference required for rigorous synthesis in primary research. If primary researchers must specify quantitatively the relation of the data to their conclusions, the next users of the data should be required to do the same.

A Brief History of Meta-Analysis

Gene Glass (1976) introduced the term *meta-analysis* to stand for the statistical analysis of results from individual studies "for purposes of integrating the findings" (p. 3). Procedures for performing meta-analysis had existed long before 1976. Indeed, methods for combining results of independent studies date back to the 1930s (Fisher, 1932; Pearson, 1933), but instances of their application were rare. It took the expanding data base and the growing need for research reviews to provide impetus for the general use of meta-analysis.

Meta-analysis was not without its critics. The value of quantitative reviewing was questioned along lines similar to criticisms of primary data analysis (e.g., Mansfield & Bussey, 1977; Barber, 1978). However, much of the criticism stemmed less from issues in meta-analysis than from more general inappropriate reviewing procedures (such as a lack of operational detail) that were erroneously linked to it (see Cooper & Arkin, 1981).

Evidence indicates that meta-analysis is now an accepted procedure, and its application within the social sciences continues to grow. According to Guzzo, Jackson, and Katzell (1987), the number of articles and dissertations in *Psychological Abstracts* that were indexed under "meta-analysis" reached nearly 100 in 1985. Greenberg and Folger (1988) state that "if the current interest in meta-analysis is any indication, then meta-analysis is here to stay" (p. 191).

When Not to Use Statistics

Much of this chapter will examine the quantitative reviewing procedures that are available and how they are applied. It is important, however, to state explicitly some circumstances in which the use of quantitative procedures in reviews is *not* appropriate.

First, the basic premise behind the use of statistics in reviews is that *a series of studies have been identified that address an identical conceptual hypothesis.* If the premises of a review do not include this assertion, then there is no need for cumulative statistics. Quantitative procedures are applicable only to integrative research reviews, not to reviews with other focuses or goals (see Chapter 1). For instance, if a reviewer is interested in tracing the historical development of the concept of hyperactivity, it would not be necessary for him or her to do a quantitative review. However, if the reviewer also intends to make an inference about whether or not different definitions of hyperactivity (i.e., methods of diagnosis) lead to differing effectiveness for drug treatments, then a quantitative summary of relevant research would be appropriate.

The drug treatment of hyperactivity illustrative review points out a second limitation on quantitative syntheses. In this review, separate analyses were conducted on comparisons of drug treatment versus placebo control groups and drug treatment versus no-treatment control groups. Even though both comparisons assessed the effectiveness of drugs, it would not necessarily be informative to lump them together. When a hypothesis involves a comparison with controls, the reviewer might find that a distinction in the type of control is important enough not to be obscured by a quantitative analysis.

Third, a reviewer should not quantitatively combine studies at a broader conceptual level than readers would find useful. At an extreme, most social science research could be categorized as examining a single conceptual hypothesis—social stimuli affect human behavior. Indeed, for some purposes, such a hypothesis test might be very enlightening. However, this should not be used as an excuse to lump together concepts and hypotheses without attention to those distinctions that will be meaningful to the users of the review (see Kazdin,

Durac, & Agteros, 1979, for a humorous treatment of this issue). For instance, the review of personality moderators of interpersonal expectancy effects provides an example of when a quantitative combination of studies was possible but not profitable. A total of 33 studies were found that tested the broad conceptual hypothesis. Of those, 24 (contained in 17 reports) examined experimenter expectancy effects on photo-rating tasks, 6 used other laboratory settings, 1 used an instructional setting, and 2 used simulated therapeutic settings. Yet, rather than lump them all together, only the studies on photo-rating tasks were meta-analyzed. To have accumulated results at any broader conceptual level and to have claimed general ecological validity based on this cumulation would have been misleading, since over two-thirds of all comparisons were conducted in highly specific settings.

Integrating Techniques and Differences in Review Outcomes

While the relative validity of different inference strategies is difficult to assess, Cooper and Rosenthal (1980) did demonstrate some of the objective differences between quantitative and nonquantitative procedures in research reviews. Graduate students and faculty were asked to evaluate a literature on a simple question: Is gender related to task persistence? All reviewers evaluated the same set of studies, but half the reviewers used quantitative procedures and half used whatever criteria appealed to them. No reviewer in the latter condition chose quantitative techniques. Statistical reviewers reported more support for the hypothesis and a larger relationship between variables than did nonstatistical reviewers. Statistical reviewers also tended to view future replicative research as less necessary than did nonstatistical reviewers, although this finding did not reach statistical significance.

It is also likely that the different statistical tests employed by reviewers who adopt quantitative procedures will create variance in review conclusions. Several different paradigms have emerged for quantitatively reviewing social science research with a parametric model (Glass et al., 1981; Hedges & Olkin, 1985; Hunter, Schmidt, & Jackson, 1982; Rosenthal, 1984), and other paradigms can be used with a Bayesian perspective (Raudenbush & Bryk, 1985; Viana, 1980). There are numerous techniques available for combining the separate study probabilities to generate an overall probability for the run of studies (Rosenthal, 1984). The different techniques generate probability levels that vary somewhat. Thus the rules adopted to carry out quantitative analysis can differ from reviewer to reviewer, and this may create variance in how review results are interpreted. We can assume as well that the rules used by nonquantitative reviewers also vary, but their unexplicit nature makes them difficult to compare formally.

SYNTHESIZING MAIN EFFECTS AND INTERACTIONS

Before examining several of the quantitative techniques available to reviewers, it is important to take a closer look at some of the distinct features of accumulated tests of hypotheses. In the chapter on problem formulation, it was pointed out that at first most research reviews focus on tests of main effects. This is primarily because conceptually identical tests of main effects have occurred more frequently than tests of three or more interacting variables. Of course, once the reviewer has discerned whether or not a main effect is present, he or she next turns to potential moderators of the relation or to interaction hypotheses.

In research reviews the principal feature of both main effect and interaction tests is that the significance levels and relationship strengths associated with separate tests of the same hypothesis will vary from one testing to the next, and this variability is sometimes dramatic.

Variability in Main Effect Tests

Varying results for tests of main effects can be produced because of two classes of reasons. Perhaps the simplest cause is the one most often over-looked—sampling error. Taveggia (1974) made the point well:

> A methodological principle overlooked by writers of . . . reviews is that research results are *probabilistic*. What this principle suggests is that, in and of themselves, the findings of any single research are meaningless—they may have occurred simply by chance. It also follows that if a large enough number of researches has been done on a particular topic, chance alone dictates that studies will exist that report inconsistent and contradictory findings! Thus, what appears to be contradictory may simply be the positive and negative details of a distribution of findings. (pp. 397-398)

Taveggia highlights one of the implications of using probability theory and sampling techniques to make inferences about populations. As an example, suppose it were possible to measure the academic achievement of every American student. Also, suppose that if such a task were undertaken, it would be found that achievement was exactly equal for students who do homework and those who do not—that is, exactly equal group means existed for the two populations. Still, if 1,000 samples of 50 homeworkers and 50 no-homeworkers were taken and the sample means were compared using the $p < .05$ significance level (two-tailed), about 25 comparisons would show a significant difference favoring homeworkers while about 25 favored no-homeworkers. This variation in results is an unavoidable consequence of the fact that the means estimated by the samples will vary somewhat from the true population values. Therefore, just by chance some comparisons will pair sample estimates that vary from their true population values by large amounts and in opposite directions.

In the example given, it is unlikely that the reviewer would be fooled into thinking anything but chance caused the result—after all, 950 comparisons would reveal null effects and significant results would be distributed equally for both possible outcomes. In practical applications, however, the pattern of results is rarely this clear: First, as was pointed out in the chapter on study retrieval, the reviewer might not be aware of all null findings because they are hard to find. Also, even if an overall relation does exist between two variables (that is, the null hypothesis is false), some studies can still show significant results in a direction opposite to the overall conclusion. To continue the example, if the average achievement of homeworkers is greater than that of no-homeworkers, it is still possible that some samplings will favor no-homeworkers, depending on the size of the relation and the number of comparisons performed. In sum, one source of variance in the results of studies can be chance fluctuations due to the inexactness of sampled estimates.

A second source of variance in main effects is typically of more interest to reviewers: the differences in results created by variations in how studies are conducted and/or who participates in them. For instance, it might be that in the entire population, the difference between achievement among students who do and don't do homework is greater in high school than in elementary school. In Chapter 2, the notion of review-generated evidence for relations was introduced to describe the procedure of examining how study characteristics associate with variation in study results.

That two sources of variance in research results exist raises an interesting dilemma for the reviewer. When so-called contradictory findings occur, should the reviewer seek an explanation for them by attempting to identify differences among the methods used in studies? Or should the reviewer simply write off the contradictory findings as produced by chance variations due to sampling error? Some tests have been devised to help reviewers answer this question. In effect these tests use "sampling error" as the null hypothesis. If the variation in results across studies is too great to be explained by sampling error, then the reviewer knows to seek explanations elsewhere, that is, in methodological differences between studies. For now, however, it should simply be noted that these two distinct sources of variance in study results need to be considered by reviewers.

Variability in Interaction Tests

Obviously, the factors that create variability in main effects can also affect variability in tests of interaction. Interaction effects are as susceptible to sampling error and procedural variation as main effects. However, examining interactions in research reviews presents some unique problems. For ease of presentation, these will be discussed in regard to tests of two-way interactions, but the remarks generalize to higher-order interactions as well.

Figure 5.1 illustrates the results of two hypothetical studies demonstrating interactions. In Study I, the hyperactivity levels of two samples of children are examined. Drug intervention and control conditions are compared on the first day and the seventh day of treatment. On Day 1 children receiving drug treatment are less hyperactive than control children, but on Day 7 those children receiving drug treatment are considerably more hyperactive than those not receiving drug treatment. Thus the effect of the drug treatment on hyperactivity reverses itself over the course of the study.

In hypothetical Study II, on Day 1 children receiving the drug treatment are less hyperactive than children in the control group, but on Day 5 no difference between the drug and control group is found. Here the effect of the drug treatment "disappears" between the first and second measurement of hyperactivity.

A reviewer uncovering two studies with these findings might be tempted at first glance to conclude that they produced inconsistent results. Study I indicates that drug treatments are initially effective, but with the passage of time they actually become counterproductive. Study II evidences no counterproductive effect, just a vanishing of the desired result. A closer examination of the two figures, however, reveals why it might not be appropriate to conclude that the studies are inconsistent. The results of Study II probably would have been closely approximated by the researchers in Study I if they had taken a measurement of hyperactivity on Day 5. Likewise, had Study II contained a Day 7 measurement, these researchers probably would have produced results quite similar to the Day 7 results contained in Study I. In general, researchers who find the experimental effect appears at only one level of an interacting variable can only speculate about whether or not sampling from more extended levels of that variable would have led to a crisscrossing of the effects. Research reviewers, however, may have an opportunity to draw such conclusions more confidently.

As the example demonstrates, the research reviewer must not assume that different forms or strengths of interaction uncovered by different studies necessarily imply an inconsistency of results. Instead, research reviewers need to examine the differing levels of variables employed in different studies and if possible to chart results taking the different variable levels into account. In this manner one of the benefits of research reviewing is realized. While one study suggests that the effect of a drug on hyperactivity dissipates over time and another study suggests that the drug effect reverses itself over time, the research reviewer can find that the two results are in fact perfectly commensurate.

This possibility also underscores the importance of primary researchers presenting detailed information concerning the levels of variables used in their studies. Without specific information research reviewers may not be able to conduct an across-study analysis similar to the one presented above. If the primary researchers in Study I and Study II neglected to specify how long a delay was used between measurements, perhaps referring to the two measure-

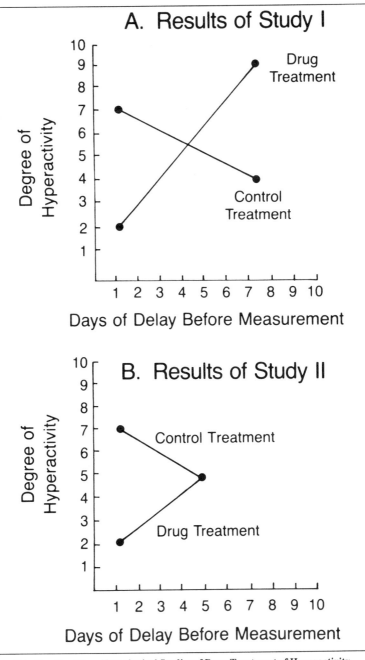

Figure 5.1: Results of Two Hypothetical Studies of Drug Treatment of Hyperactivity

ment intervals as, say, "short" and "long," the commensurability of the results would have been impossible to demonstrate.

Research reviewers must also carefully examine the statistical analyses that accompany reports of interactions. For instance, all else being equal, it is more likely that the researchers of Study I reported a significant interaction between time of measurement and treatment than did the researchers in Study II. In fact, assuming equal error terms, the F-value in Study I for the interaction should be several times greater than that in Study II.

In sum, it is extremely important that reviewers retrieve the most detailed data about interactions regardless of statistical significance. The problem, of course, is that unless the interaction was the chief concern of the primary researchers or the interaction proved significant, there is little likelihood that information detailed enough to perform the kind of analysis portrayed in Figure 5.1 will be contained in the report.

Interactions in Quantitative Reviews

The statistical combination of interactions in quantitative reviews is a very complex task. In fact, reviews rarely combine the statistical results of studies examining the same interaction (in the personality and experimenter expectancy study, a measure of expectancy effect was first devised and the main effect of personality on it was analyzed; see Zuckerman, DePaulo, & Rosenthal, 1981, for an interaction example). This is due partly to the infrequency with which studies have tested the same interaction and partly to the incomplete reporting of many tests of interaction.

There are two different ways that interactions could be statistically combined across studies. First, the separate p-levels and relationship strengths associated with each study's interaction test could be aggregated. An alternative strategy would be to aggregate separately the relation of two variables at each level of the third variable. For instance, a hyperactivity review could generate an estimate of the treatment effect by aggregating all measures taken with a one-day delay and compare this to an aggregation of all measures taken with a seven-day delay. This would probably be more useful and easily interpretable to readers than a direct estimate of the magnitude of the interaction effect. However, it is rare for primary research reports to contain the information needed to isolate the different simple main effects.

TECHNIQUES FOR COMBINING PROBABILITIES
OF INDEPENDENT STUDIES

In this section and several that follow, brief introductions to some of the quantitative techniques that are available to reviewers will be presented. The techniques were chosen because of their simplicity and broad applicability. The treatment of each technique will be conceptual and introductory. The reader who wants a fuller description of the techniques covered as well as many techniques not mentioned is advised to consult the primary sources cited in the text. For the discussion that follows, it is assumed the reader has a working knowledge of the basic statistical concepts and methods employed in the social sciences.

A major reason statistical techniques are used in research reviews is to combine the probability levels associated with separate comparisons to generate an overall probability relating to the existence of a relation. For instance, if three tests of a relation find statistically significant results and seven find null results, what is the reviewer to conclude? The techniques for combining probabilities allow the reviewer to synthesize the results of numerous tests so that overall conclusions can be drawn.

Three assumptions are crucial to the validity of a conclusion based on a cumulation of individual comparisons. First and most obviously, the individual comparisons that go into a cumulative analysis should all test the same conceptual hypothesis. Regardless of how conceptually broad or narrow the idea might be, the reviewer should be comfortable with the assertion that all the included comparisons address the same question.

Second, the separate comparisons that go into the cumulative analysis must be independent of one another. Identifying independent comparisons was discussed in the chapter on data evaluation. The quantitative reviewer must take care to identify comparisons so that it can be argued that each one contains unique information about the hypothesis.

Finally, the reviewer must believe that the initial assumptions made by the primary researchers to compute the results of the comparison were valid. Thus if the reviewer wishes to combine the probabilities associated with a series of t-test comparisons, he or she must assume that the observations, residuals, or errors of the two groups are independent and normally distributed and that the variances are roughly equal.

Vote Counting Methods

The simplest methods for combining results of independent comparisons are the vote counting methods. Vote counts can be done on the direction of the results of comparisons or on the frequency of statistically significant findings.

To do a vote count of directional results, the reviewer must first count the number of comparisons that report results in one direction (called *positive*, for presentation purposes) and compare this to the number of comparisons reporting results in the other direction (called *negative*). In this analysis the reviewer ignores the statistical significance of the separate findings. Once the number of results in each direction is counted, the reviewer performs a sign test to discover if the cumulative results suggest that one direction occurs more frequently than chance would suggest. If the null hypothesis is true—that is, if no relation between the variables under consideration exists in the population sampled by any study—we would expect the number of findings in each direction to be equal.

The formula for computing the sign test is as follows:

$$Z_{vc} = \frac{(N_p) - (\frac{1}{2} \times N_t)}{\frac{1}{2}\sqrt{N_t}} \qquad [1]$$

where

Z_{vc} = the standard normal deviate, or Z-score, for the overall series of comparisons;

N_p = the number of positive findings; and

N_t = the total number of comparisons (positive plus negative findings).

The Z_{vc} can be referred to a table of standard normal deviates to discover the probability (one-tailed) associated with the cumulative set of directional findings. If a two-tailed p-level is desired, the tabled value should be doubled. The values of Z associated with different p-levels are presented in Table 5.1.

For example, if 25 of 36 comparisons find results in the positive direction, the probability that the positive and negative directions have an equal chance to occur in the population is p < .02 (two-tailed; $Z_{vc} = 2.33$). Therefore, this result would lead the reviewer to conclude that a positive relation was supported by the series of studies.

A practical problem with the directional vote count is that primary researchers frequently do not report the direction of results, especially if a comparison proves statistically nonsignificant. An alternative vote counting method is to perform a sign test on the frequency of only statistically significant results reported in the positive direction versus the frequency of significant results reported in the negative direction. In performing this procedure, the reviewer assumes that under the null hypothesis of no relation in the population of any study, the frequency of significant positive and that of negative results (in the null case, type I errors) are expected to be equal (Hedges & Olkin, 1980). The reviewer should bear in mind, however, that the number of nonsignificant findings under the null assumption is expected to be much greater than the number of either positive or negative significant findings. Therefore, it is *not* legitimate to test for equal frequencies across the three classes of outcomes (positive, negative, and nonsignificant findings). Hedges and Olkin (1980) have shown that if a reviewer makes the assumption that when no relation exists in the population the number of positive, negative, *and* null findings will be equal, then the vote count method is extremely conservative (that is, likely to miss relations that exist). For instance, assume that a correlation of r = +.30 exists between two variables in a population and 20 comparisons have been conducted,

TABLE 5.1
Standard Normal Deviate Distribution

γ	$\alpha'' = 1 - \gamma$	$\alpha' = \frac{1}{2}(1 - \gamma)$	z
.995	.005	.0025	2.807
.99	.01	.005	2.576
.985	.015	.0075	2.432
.98	.02	.01	2.326
.975	.025	.0125	2.241
.97	.03	.015	2.170
.965	.035	.0175	2.108
.96	.04	.02	2.054
.954	.046	.023	2.000
.95	.05	.025	1.960
.94	.06	.03	1.881
.92	.08	.04	1.751
.9	.1	.05	1.645
.85	.15	.075	1.440
.8	.2	.10	1.282
.75	.25	.125	1.150
.7	.3	.150	1.036
.6	.4	.20	0.842
.5	.5	.25	0.674
.4	.6	.30	0.524
.3	.7	.35	0.385
.2	.8	.40	0.253
.1	.9	.45	0.126

γ = area between $-z$ and z
   = confidence coefficient

$\alpha' = \frac{1}{2}(1 - \gamma)$

   = area above z
   = area above $-z$
   = significance level for one-sided test

$\alpha'' = 1 - \gamma = 2\alpha'$

   = area beyond $-z$ and z
   = significance level for two-sided test

SOURCE: Reprinted with permission from Noether (1971).

with 40 people in each comparison. The chance that the vote count associated with this series of studies will be significant if the assumption of equal numbers of each finding is used is only p = .059!

   Adjusting the expected frequencies of the three findings so that the disproportionate number of expected nonsignificant findings is taken into account solves the theoretical problem but raises a practical one. We have seen that null results are less likely to be reported by researchers and thus are less likely to be retrieved by reviewers. Therefore, if the appropriate theoretical values are used in a vote count analysis, it should often occur that both positive and negative results appear *more* frequently than expected. Thus it seems that using the frequency of nonsignificant findings in a vote count procedure is of dubious value.

In sum, then, a reviewer can perform vote counts to aggregate results across individual studies by comparing the number of "raw" directional findings or the number of significant findings in the two directions. Both of these procedures will be conservative (i.e., will miss relations that exist) because much information will be lost—the raw direction of results will not appear in many research reports in one case and nonsignificant findings cannot contribute to the analysis in the other case. Vote counts should always be described in quantitative reviews but should be used to draw inferences only when the number of studies to be aggregated is large and should always be supplemented with more sensitive procedures.

Combining Significance Tests

Rosenthal (1978b) cataloged seven different methods for cumulating results that use as their basic data the precise probability values associated with each comparison. The simplest and most routinely applicable of the seven methods will be presented here. The method, called Adding Zs by Rosenthal, was first introduced by Stouffer in 1949.

The Adding Zs method uses the following formula:

$$Z_{st} = \frac{\sum_{i=1}^{N} Z_i}{\sqrt{N}} \qquad [2]$$

where

Z_{st} = the standard normal deviate, or Z-score, for the overall series of comparisons;

Z_i = the standard normal deviate for the ith comparison; and

N = the total number of comparisons in the series.

The steps for carrying out the analysis are simple. The reviewer must

(1) choose which direction for the hypothesis will be considered positive and which negative;

(2) record the probability associated with each comparison;

(3) if the reported probability is two-tailed, halve it;

(4) look up the Z-score associated with each probability;

(5) sum the Z-scores, remembering to place a minus sign before negative results; and

(6) divide this sum by the square root of the number of comparisons.

The resulting Z_{st} can then be referred to a table of standard normal deviates (see Table 5.1) to discover the probability associated with the cumulative set of individual probabilities. If a two-tailed probability is desired, the tabled p-level should be doubled. The probability describes the combined likelihood that the series of results included in the analysis could have been generated by chance if the null hypothesis were true for every study.

Table 5.2 presents a hypothetical application of the Adding Zs method. Note that hypothetical Studies 2 and 7 produced exact null results (probably due to inexact reporting). Studies 1 and 5 produced statistically significant results, and Study 4 produced a result opposite to that predicted.

The method of Adding Zs can be modified to allow the reviewer to weight the results of different comparisons differentially (see Mosteller & Bush, 1954; Rosenthal, 1978b). For instance, if several comparisons come from a single study, the reviewer might want to weight these less than another comparison that is the only contribution of another study. Or the reviewer might want to give added weight to studies based on larger sample sizes.

The formula for the Adding Weighted Zs method is:

$$Z_w = \frac{\sum_{i=1}^{N} W_i Z_i}{\sqrt{\sum_{i=1}^{N} W_i^2}} \qquad [3]$$

where

Z_w = the Z-score for the weighted combination of studies;

W_i = the weighting factor associated with each study; and all other terms are defined as before.

Table 5.2 presents a hypothetical example of the Adding Weighted Zs method, with the weighting factor being the sample size of the study.

The Fail-safe N

It has been mentioned several times that not all comparisons have an equal likelihood of being retrieved by the reviewer. Nonsignificant results are less likely to be retrieved than significant ones. This fact implies that the Adding Zs method may produce a probability level (chance of a type I error) that is an underestimate. Rosenthal (1979a) wrote, "The extreme view of this problem . . . is that the journals are filled with the 5% of studies that show Type I errors, while the file drawers back in the lab are filled with the 95% of studies that show

TABLE 5.2
Hypothetical Example of the Combination of Eight Comparisons

Study	Number of Participants (N)	N^2	One-Tailed p-Level	Associated Z-Score	NZ
1	48	2304	.025	1.96	94.08
2	28	784	.50	0	0
3	32	1024	.33	.44	14.08
4	24	576	.90	−1.28	−30.72
5	64	4096	.01	2.33	149.12
6	40	1600	.39	.28	11.20
7	20	400	.50	0	0
8	30	900	.15	1.04	31.20
Σ	286	11684		4.77	268.96

Adding Zs: $Z_{st} = \dfrac{4.77}{\sqrt{8}} = 1.69,\ p < .0461$, one-tailed

Adding Weighted Zs: $Z_w = \dfrac{268.96}{\sqrt{11684}} = 2.49,\ p < .0064$, one-tailed

$N_{FS.05} = \left(\dfrac{4.77}{1.645}\right)^2 - 8 = .41$ (or 1)

NOTE: The one-tailed p-level of .90 is from a study finding a direction opposite to that predicted (thus the associated Z-score is negative).

insignificant (e.g., p < .05) results" (p. 638). The problem is probably not this dramatic, but it does exist.

One of the advantages of the Adding Zs method is that it allows the calculation of a Fail-safe N (see Cooper, 1979; Rosenthal, 1979a). The Fail-safe N answers the question, "How many comparisons totaling to a null hypothesis confirmation (e.g., $Z_{st} = 0$) would have to be added to the results of the retrieved comparisons in order to change the conclusion that a relation exists?" Rosenthal (1979a) called this the "tolerance for future null results." The formula for calculating this number, when the chosen significance level is p < .05, is as follows:

$$N_{FS.05} = \left(\frac{\sum_{i=1}^{N} Z_i}{1.645} \right)^2 - N \qquad [4]$$

where

$N_{FS.05}$ = the number of additional null-summing comparisons needed to raise the combined probability of just above p < .05;

1.645 = the standard normal deviate associated with p < .05 (one-tailed); and all other quantities are defined as before.

Obviously, the Fail-safe N cannot be computed when studies are weighted unequally, unless the reviewer wishes to estimate what the average weight of unretrieved comparisons might be—a dubious estimate at best. A hypothetical example of a Fail-safe N is presented in Table 5.2.

The Fail-safe N is a valuable descriptive statistic. It allows the users of a review to evaluate the cumulative result of the review against their assessment of how exhaustively the reviewer has searched the literature. However, the Fail-safe N also contains an assumption that restricts its validity. That is, its user must find credible the proposition that the sum of the unretrieved studies is equal to an exact null result. It might be the case that unretrieved studies have a cumulative result opposite to that contained in the review—perhaps because primary researchers did not want to publish studies that contradicted studies already in print. Or unretrieved studies might cumulatively add support to the conclusion because the reviewer ignored information channels that paralleled those that were used. The plausibility of these alternatives should always be assessed when a Fail-safe N is interpreted.

When is a Fail-safe N large enough so that reviewers and readers can conclude a finding is resistant to unretrieved null results? Rosenthal (1979b) suggests that the resistance number equal 5 times the number of retrieved studies plus 10. No steadfast rule is intuitively obvious, so reviewers should argue anew for the resistance of their findings each time the formula is applied. The best argument for a resistant finding is a large Fail-safe N coupled with a comprehensive search strategy.

Combining Raw Data

The most desirable technique for combining results of independent studies is to integrate the raw data from each relevant comparison. The separate data points can be placed into an analysis of variance or multiple regression that employs the comparison that generated the data as a blocking variable. Obviously, instances in which the integration of raw data can be achieved are rare. Raw data are seldom included in research reports and attempts to obtain raw data from researchers often end in failure (see Chapter 4).

The benefits of integrating raw data can also be achieved, however, if the reviewer has access to the means and standard deviations associated with each comparison. A problem with the use of means and standard deviations is that the dependent variable measurements in the separate comparisons are often not commensurate with one another—that is, they use different instruments with different ranges of values. Of course, the reviewer can standardize the measurements in each comparison to make them commensurate. Again, however, the reporting of individual group means and standard deviations in primary research reports is infrequent, though certainly not as rare as the reporting of raw data.

In sum, analyzing raw data from separate comparisons is the optimum strategy for accumulating results. It is the level of analysis to which the reviewer should aspire and its feasibility should be assessed before other less adequate means for combining results are undertaken. In practice, however, the use of this technique is rare.

Combined Results and Study-Generated Evidence

In Chapter 2 the distinction between study-generated and review-generated evidence was discussed. It was pointed out that study-generated evidence is present when a single study contains results that directly test the relation being considered. The results of the cumulative analysis techniques presented thus far produce study-generated evidence. That is, each individual comparison being integrated has something to say about the hypothesis under consideration. Therefore, if the individual comparisons have used random assignment of participants to conditions in order to uncover causal mechanisms, the combined results of these comparisons relate to those causal mechanisms. Based on vote counts and combined probabilities, the reviewer can make assertions about causality if in fact the primary research included experimental manipulations. A similar assertion cannot be made about the evidence generated by an examination of research methods that covary with results, a topic to be pursued shortly.

The illustrative reviews. The review of personality moderators of interpersonal expectancy effects in laboratory experiments calculated five combined Z-scores and probabilities, one for each hypothesis. The study was used as the unit of analysis and each study was weighted equally. It was found that experimenters with a greater need for social influence were more likely to generate interpersonal expectancy effects. The combined Z-score, based on eight studies, was 2.94 with an associated p-level of .0032, two-tailed. The Fail-safe N, the number of null-summing studies needed to raise the combined probability to above p = .05 (two-tailed), was 10.02, or 11 (since 10 studies would be just below p = .05).

Tests of the expressiveness and likability of the experimenter indicated nonsignificant relations to experimenter bias, though in both cases the relation was positive (for expressiveness, N = 3, Z = 1.79. p < .0734, two-tailed; for likability, N = 4, Z = 1.71, p < .0872, two-tailed). The influenceability and decoding skills of the subject were both positively related to the appearance of expectancy effects (for influenceability, N = 11, Z = 2.21, p < .027, two-tailed; for decoding skill, N = 7, Z = 2.60, p < .0094, two-tailed).

The review of research design effects on response rates to questionnaires presented a rare opportunity to combine raw data. All of the 93 relevant studies reported their raw data. In this case, the raw data consisted of the number of persons contacted and the number who responded. In addition, in all studies the dependent variable, response or nonresponse, was identical. For instance, 8,577 people participated in studies that experimentally manipulated whether or not a monetary incentive was offered for responding to the questionnaire. Of these, 55.5% of participants who were offered a monetary incentive returned the questionnaire, while 35.2% of participants not offered an incentive returned the questionnaire. The chi-square value associated with these figures is 188.1, a highly significant value. The proportions used in these analyses were weighted by the number of persons contacted in each study. Thus those studies with larger samples contributed more to this overall result than studies that contained small samples.

MEASURING RELATIONSHIP STRENGTH

The primary function of the statistical procedures described above is to help the reviewer accept or reject the null hypothesis. The null hypothesis, of course, tests the "no relation in any study" hypothesis against all others. Most primary researchers have been content simply to identify hypotheses with some explanatory value—that is, to reject the null. The prevalence of this yes-or-no question is partly due to the relatively recent development of the social sciences. Social hypotheses are crudely stated first approximations to the truth. How potent variables are for explaining human behavior and how competing explanations compare with regard to relative potency are questions that have rarely been asked. As theoretical sophistication has increased, however, more social scientists are making inquiries about the size of relations.

Giving further impetus to the "How much?" question is a growing disenchantment with the null hypothesis significance test itself. Whether or not a null hypothesis can be rejected is tied closely to the particular research project under scrutiny. As mentioned earlier, if an ample number of participants are available or if a sensitive research design is employed, a rejection of the null hypothesis is not surprising. In research reviews this fact becomes even more apparent.

A null hypothesis rejection, then, does not guarantee that an important social insight has been achieved. This point was made by David Lykken (1968): "Statistical significance is perhaps the least important attribute of a good experiment. It is never a sufficient condition for claiming that a theory has been usefully corroborated, that a meaningful empirical fact has been established, or that an experimental report ought to be published" (p. 151). Answering the question "How much?" allows a considerably more informed judgment about explanatory value than does answering the question, "Is it different from zero?" And, as we shall see shortly, the latter question can be answered by placing a confidence interval around our "How much?" estimate, obviating the need for combined probabilities.

A Definition of Effect Size

In order to answer the "How much?" question meaningfully, a definition for the notion of relationship strength, or what is more often called the effect size (ES), must be agreed upon. Also, we need methods for quantitatively expressing the magnitude of a relation. Jacob Cohen, in *Statistical Power Analysis for the Behavioral Sciences* (1988), presents a very thorough and useful examination of the definition of effect sizes (also see Lipsey, in press). Cohen defines an effect size as follows:

> Without intending any necessary implication of causality, it is convenient to use the phrase "effect size" to mean "the *degree* to which the phenomenon is present in the population," or "the degree to which the null hypothesis is false." By the above route it can now readily be clear that when the null hypothesis is false, it is false to some specific degree, i.e., *the effect size (ES) is some specific non-zero value in the population*. The larger this value, the greater the *degree* to which the phenomenon under study is manifested. (pp. 9-10)

Figure 5.2 presents three hypothetical relationships that illustrate Cohen's definition. Suppose the illustrated results come from three experiments comparing a drug treatment of hyperactivity with a placebo. Figure 5.2A presents a null relationship. That is, the sampled children given the drug have a mean and distribution of hyperactivity scores identical to the placebo-treated children. In Figure 5.2B the treated children have a mean slightly higher than that of the placebo children, and in Figure 5.2C, the difference between treatments is even greater. A measure of effect size must express the three results so that greater departures from the null are associated with higher effect size values.

Cohen's book contains many different metrics for describing the strength of a relation. Each effect size index is associated with a particular research design in a manner similar to t-tests being associated with two-group comparisons, F-tests associated with multigroup designs, and chi-squares associated with frequency tables. The two primary metrics and one secondary metric for describing relationship strength will be presented below. These metrics are generally useful—almost any research outcome can be expressed using one of them. For more detailed information on these effect size metrics, as well as many others, the reader should consult Cohen (1988). However, it is strongly advised that both primary researchers and research reviewers not use effect estimates for multiple degree of freedom tests, even though Cohen lists several of them. All effect sizes should be expressed (1) as comparisons between two groups, (2) as measures of correlation between two continuous variables, or (3) as other single degree of freedom contrasts if multiple groups are involved. The reasoning behind this qualification is simple. In an analysis of variance a multiple degree of freedom F-test tells whether there is significant variability in the array of group means, but it does not tell which groups vary significantly from one another. Therefore, in all instances it is essential that multiple degree of freedom significance tests be followed by single degree of freedom comparisons. The same would be true for the effect sizes associated with these tests. If the primary researcher or research reviewer defines the problem precisely, he or she should be able to identify single degree of freedom inference tests and associated effect sizes for each comparison of interest. Thus the following discussion is restricted to metrics commensurate with single degree of freedom tests.

The d-Index

The d-index of an effect size is appropriate when the means of two groups are being compared. Thus the d-index is typically used in association with t-tests or F-tests based on a comparison of two conditions. The d-index expresses the distance between the two group means in terms of their common standard deviation. For example, if d = .40 it means 4/10 of a standard deviation separate the two means.

The hypothetical research results presented in Figure 5.2 will illustrate the d-index. For the research result that supports the null hypothesis (Figure 5.2A), the d-index equals zero. That is, there is no distance between the drug treatment and placebo group means. The second research result (Figure 5.2B) reveals a d-index of .40, that is, the mean of the drug treatment group lies 4/10 of a standard deviation above the placebo group's mean. In the third example, a d-index of .85 is portrayed. Here the group with the higher mean (drug treatment) has a mean that rests 85/100 of a standard deviation above the lower-meaned (placebo) group's mean.

Calculating the d-index is simple. The formula is as follows:

$$d = \frac{X_{1.} - X_{2.}}{SD} \qquad [5]$$

where

X_1 and X_2 =   the two group means and
SD   =   the average standard deviation of the two groups.

The formula for the d-index assumes that the two groups have equal (or roughly equal) standard deviations. In instances where the researcher does not wish to make the assumption that the standard deviations of the two groups are equal, the d-index can be calculated by using the standard deviation of one group or the other—typically the control group, if it is available.

The d-index is not only simple to compute, but it is also scale-free. That is, the standard deviation adjustment in the denominator of the formula means that studies using different measurement scales can be compared or combined.

In many instances reviewers will find that primary researchers do not report the means and standard deviations of the separate groups the reviewer wishes to compare. For such cases Friedman (1968) has provided a computation formula for the d-index that does not require the reviewer to have specific means and standard deviations. This formula is as follows:

$$d = \frac{2t}{\sqrt{df_{error}}} \hspace{3cm} [6]$$

where

t   =   the value of the t-test for the associated comparison and
df_{error} =   the degrees of freedom associated with the t-test.

In instances where F-tests with single degrees of freedom in the numerator are reported, the t-value in the above formula can be substituted for by the square root of the F-value ($t = \sqrt{F}$), if the sign of the mean difference is known.

The d-index may leave something to be desired in terms of its intuitive appeal. For this reason, Cohen (1988) also presents a measure associated with the d-index called U_3. U_3 tells the percentage of the sample with the lower mean that was exceeded by 50% of the scores in the higher-meaned group. Put more informally, U_3 answers the question, "What percentage of the scores in the lower-meaned group was exceeded by the average score in the higher-meaned group?" Values for converting the d-index to U_3 are presented in Table 5.3. For example, the d-index of .40 presented in Figure 5.2B has an associated U_3 value of 65.5%. This means that 65.5% of the scores in the lower-meaned (placebo) group are exceeded by the average score in the higher-meaned (drug treatment) group. For Figure 5.2C, the d-index of .85 is associated with a U_3 of 80.2. Thus 80.2% of the scores in the lower-meaned (placebo) group are exceeded by the average score in the higher-meaned (drug treatment) group.

Figure 5.2: Three Hypothetical Relations Between Drug and Placebo Groups in Hyperactivity Experiments

Hedges (1980) has shown that the d-index may slightly overestimate the size of an effect in the entire population. However, the bias is minimal if the degrees of freedom associated with the t-test are more than 20. If a reviewer is calculating d-indexes from primary research based on samples smaller than 20, Hedges's (1980) correction factor should be applied.

The r-Index

A second effect size, the r-index, is simply the Pearson product-moment correlation coefficient. This index is familiar to most social scientists, but the formula for the r-index requires variances and covariances, so it can rarely be computed from information typically presented in primary research reports. Luckily, in most instances where r-indexes are applicable, primary researchers do report them. If only the t-test value associated with the r-index is given, the r-index value can be calculated using the following formula:

$$r = \sqrt{\frac{t^2}{t^2 + df_{error}}} \qquad [7]$$

Likewise, when a chi-square statistic associated with a 2 × 2 contingency table is given, the r-index can be estimated as follows:

$$r = \sqrt{\frac{\chi^2}{n.}} \qquad [8]$$

where

χ^2 = the chi-square value associated with the comparison and
n. = the total number of observations in the comparison.

Cohen distinguishes the effect size associated with chi-squares by calling it a w-index, but in fact it is identical to an r-index when df = 1.

Finally, one problem that may arise for the research reviewer is that different primary researchers may choose different metrics to study the same phenomena. For instance, in the review of the relation between personality and interpersonal expectancy effects, some primary researchers dichotomized personality variables into "high" and "low" groups and used a t-test to measure statistical significance. Other researchers left the personality scales in their continuous form and correlated them with continuous measures of expectancy effects. When this occurs the reviewer must convert one metric into the other so that a single metric can be used in the research review. Conveniently, the different effect size metrics are easily converted from one to the other. The r-index can be transformed into a d-index by the following formula:

$$d = \frac{2r}{\sqrt{1-r^2}} \qquad [9]$$

TABLE 5.3
Equivalents Among Several Measures of Effect

d	U_3	r	r^2
0	50.0%	.000	.000
.1	54.0	.050	.002
.2	57.9	.100	.010
.3	61.8	.148	.022
.4	65.5	.196	.038
.5	69.1	.243	.059
.6	72.6	.287	.083
.7	75.8	.330	.109
.8	78.8	.371	.138
.9	81.6	.410	.168
1.0	84.1	.447	.200
1.1	86.4	.482	.232
1.2	88.5	.514	.265
1.3	90.3	.545	.297
1.4	91.9	.573	.329
1.5	93.3	.600	.360
1.6	94.5	.625	.390
1.7	95.5	.648	.419
1.8	96.4	.669	.448
1.9	97.1	.689	.474
2.0	97.7	.707	.500
2.2	98.6	.740	.548
2.4	99.2	.768	.590
2.6	99.5	.793	.628
2.8	99.7	.814	.662
3.0	99.9	.832	.692
3.2	99.9	.848	.719
3.4	*	.862	.743
3.6	*	.874	.764
3.8	*	.885	.783
4.0	*	.894	.800

SOURCE: Reprinted with permission from Cohen (1988).
*Greater than 99.95.

or the d-index into the r-index by:

$$r = \frac{d}{\sqrt{d^2 + 4}}$$ [10]

Table 5.3 gives some of the equivalents among the measures of effect.

Statistical Factors Influencing the Size of Effects

In addition to the "true" impact one variable has on another, there are numerous influences on the magnitude of relations revealed in empirical research. Just a few of the more important statistical factors that may influence an effect size will be mentioned here. This introduction will largely be conceptual; for a detailed, technical discussion of these issues, the reader is advised to consult Glass et al. (1981).

The first statistical factor that will influence the magnitude of relations is the reliability of the measurements involved in the study. The less "pure" a measurement is, the less ability it has to detect relations involving the variable of interest. To estimate the impact that unreliability of measures may have on an effect size estimate in a research review, the reviewer might try to obtain the reliabilities (e.g., internal consistencies) of the various measures. These can then be used to see if effect sizes correlate with the reliability of the measures or to estimate what effect sizes would be if all measures were perfectly reliable (see Hunter et al., 1982, for details on how to perform this estimation).

A second statistical influence on effect size estimates is the choice of the standard deviation used to estimate the variance around group means. As noted above, most reviewers have no choice but to make the assumption that the two group standard deviations are equal to each other because the effect size must be estimated from an associated significance test, which also makes this assumption. However, in instances where information about standard deviations is available and they appear to be unequal, the reviewer should always choose one group's standard deviation to act as the estimate (e.g., the denominator in the d-index). If a treatment and control group are compared, the control group standard deviation should be used. For the U_3 index, this allows the reviewer to state the impact of the treatment in comparison to the untreated population, for example, "The average treated person scored higher than X% of the untreated population."

A third statistical influence on effect sizes, noted above, is the small sample bias. In addition to the bias in the effect size estimates, the reviewer should be cautious in interpreting any effect size based on small samples, for instance, when the sample size is smaller than 10. Especially when samples are small, a single extreme value can create an exceptionally large effect size estimate.

A fourth statistical influence on effect sizes is the number of factors employed in the research design. If factors other than the variable of interest are included in a research design, for instance, in an analysis of variance or a multiple regression, the reviewer is faced with the choice of employing a standard deviation estimate that has been reduced by the inclusion of the extra factors or attempting to retrieve the standard deviation that would have occurred had all the extraneous factors been ignored (i.e., been included in the error estimate). Whenever possible, the latter strategy should be employed by the reviewer; that is, an attempt should be made to calculate the effect size as though the comparison of interest were the sole comparison in the analysis. Practically speaking, however, it is often difficult for a reviewer to retrieve this overall standard deviation estimate. In such cases, the reviewer should examine whether or not the number of factors involved in the experiment is associated with the size of the experimental effect.

Combining Effect Sizes Across Studies

Once an effect size has been calculated for each study or comparison, the reviewer next averages the effects that test the same hypothesis. It is a generally accepted practice that these averages should weight the individual effect sizes based on the number of subjects in their respective samples. This is because, for example, a d-index or r-index based on 100 subjects will give a more precise and reliable estimate of the population effect size than will an estimate based on 10 subjects. The average effect size should reflect this fact.

One way to take account of sample size when calculating an average effect size is to multiply each effect by its sample size and then divide the sum of the multiplications by the sum of the sample sizes. However, there is a more precise procedure, described in detail by Hedges and Olkin (1985), that involves more complicated calculations but that has many advantages.

The d-index. For the d-index, this procedure first involves estimating a weighting factor, w_i, which is the inverse of the variance associated with each d-index estimate:

$$w_i = \frac{2(n_{i1} + n_{i2})n_{i1}n_{i2}}{2(n_{i1} + n_{i2})^2 + n_{i1}n_{i2}d_i^2} \qquad [11]$$

where

n_{i1} and n_{i2} = the number of data points in Group 1 and Group 2 of the comparison, and

d_i = the d-index of the comparison under consideration.

While the formula for w_i looks imposing, it is really a simple arithmetic manipulation of three numbers that should be available on the coding sheets. It is also easy to program a computer statistical package to perform the necessary calculation.

Table 5.4 presents the group sample sizes, d-indexes, and w's associated with seven study results. The example is drawn from actual data collected as part of the review of homework research. The seven studies each compared the effects on achievement of homework assignments that presented material only on the day the topic was covered in class with assignments that dispersed material over several days. All seven of the experiments produced results favoring dispersed homework assignments.

To demystify the weighting factor further, note that its values equal approximately half the average sample size in a group. It should not be surprising, then, that the next step in obtaining a weighted average effect size involves multiplying each d-index by its associated weight and dividing the sum of these multiplications by the sum of the weights. The formula is as follows:

$$d. = \frac{\sum\limits_{i=1}^{N} d_i w_i}{\sum\limits_{i=1}^{N} w_i} \qquad [12]$$

where all terms are defined as above. Table 5.4 shows that the average weighted d-index for the seven studies was found to be d = .115.

The advantage of using w_i over the sample sizes as weights is that w_i can be used to generate a precise confidence interval around the average effect size estimate. To do this, an estimated variance for the average effect size must be calculated. First, the inverse of the sum of the w_i's is found. Then, the square root of this variance is multiplied by the Z-score associated with the confidence interval of interest. Thus the formula for a 95% confidence interval would be as follows:

$$CId._{95\%} = d. \pm 1.96 \sqrt{\frac{1}{\sum\limits_{i=1}^{N} w_i}} \qquad [13]$$

where all terms are defined as above.

Table 5.4 reveals that the 95% confidence interval for the seven studies includes values .084 above and below the average d-index. Thus we can expect 95% of estimates of this effect to fall between d = .031 and d = .199. Note that this interval does not contain the value d = 0. It is this information that can be used to test the null hypothesis that no relation exists in the population, in place of the combined probability procedures discussed earlier. In the present instance, we would reject the null hypothesis that there was no difference in achievement between students who did current lesson only versus distributed homework.

The r-index. The procedure is simpler for finding the average weighted effect size and confidence interval when the r-index is used. Here, each r-index is first transformed to its corresponding z-score, z_i, and the following formula applied:

$$z. = \frac{\sum\limits_{i=1}^{N} (n_{i.} - 3) z_i}{\sum\limits_{i=1}^{N} (n_{i.} - 3)} \qquad [14]$$

TABLE 5.4
Example of d-Index Estimation and Tests of Homogeneity

Study	n_{i1}	n_{i2}	d_i	w_i	d_i^2/w_i	d_i/w_i	Q_b Grouping
1	259	265	.02	130.98	.052	2.619	A
2	57	62	.07	29.68	.145	2.078	A
3	43	50	.24	22.95	1.322	5.509	A
4	230	228	.11	114.32	1.383	12.576	A
5	296	291	.09	146.59	1.187	13.193	B
6	129	131	.32	64.17	6.571	20.536	B
7	69	74	.17	35.58	1.028	6.048	B
Σ	1083	1101	1.02	544.27	11.69	62.56	

$d = 62.56/544.27 = +.115$

$CI_{d.95\%} = .115 \pm 1.96\sqrt{\dfrac{1}{544.27}} = .115 \pm .084$

$Q_t = 11.69 - \dfrac{62.56^2}{544.27} = 4.5$

$Q_w = 1.16 + 2.36 = 3.52$

$Q_b = 4.5 - 3.52 = .98$

where n_i. = the total sample size for the ith comparison and all other terms are defined as above.

For the confidence interval, the formula is as follows:

$$CI_{z.95\%} = z. \pm \frac{1.96}{\sqrt{\sum_{i=1}^{N} (n_{i.} - 3)}} \qquad [15]$$

where all terms are defined as above.

Table 5.5 presents the r-to-z transformations needed to carry out the procedures. Once the confidence interval has been established, the reviewer can refer back to Table 5.5 to retrieve the corresponding r-indexes (the average r and the limits of the confidence interval).

Table 5.6 presents an example of how average r-indexes are calculated. The data are given for six comparisons correlating the amount of time a student reports spending on homework and the student's achievement level. These data are also a modification of an actual data set. The average z_i was .207, with the 95% confidence interval ranging from .195 to .219. Note that this confidence interval is quite narrow. This is because the sample sizes upon which the effect size estimates are based are large. Note also that the r-to-z transforms result in only minor changes in two of the r-index values. This would not be the case had the r-indexes been larger (e.g., an r-index of .60 is transformed to a z of .69; see Table 5.5). As with the earlier example, r = 0 is not contained in the confidence interval. Therefore, we can reject the null hypothesis that there is no relation between the amount of time students report spending on homework and their level of achievement.

The illustrative reviews. Both effect sizes presented above appeared in the illustrative reviews.

The review of drug treatments of hyperactivity revealed three separate general results. For comparisons between drug treatments and no placebo controls, the mean d-index equaled +1.21. A d-index of this magnitude indicates that the average child in the control group was more hyperactive than 88.5% of the children receiving drug treatment. The d-index for comparisons of drug treatments versus placebo controls was d = .84, or U_3 = 79.9%. For the placebo versus no-placebo control comparisons, the d-index was .32 and U_3 was 62.5%.

The r-index was used to measure effect size in the review of the relation between personality and interpersonal expectancy effects in laboratory experiments. The largest average correlation, r = +.15, was found between an experimenter's need for social influence and the generation of interpersonal expectancy effects.

Finally, the effect sizes uncovered in the review of research design effects on response rates to questionnaires were expressed using the r-index (or w-index, according to Cohen's terminology). In this case, however, the effect size was not computed by averaging the effects found in separate studies. Instead,

TABLE 5.5
Transformation of r to z

r	z	r	z	r	z	r	z	r	z
.000	.000	.200	.203	.400	.424	.600	.693	.800	1.099
.005	.005	.205	.208	.405	.430	.605	.701	.805	1.113
.010	.010	.210	.213	.410	.436	.610	.709	.810	1.127
.015	.015	.215	.218	.415	.442	.615	.717	.815	1.142
.020	.020	.220	.224	.420	.448	.620	.725	.820	1.157
.025	.025	.225	.229	.425	.454	.625	.733	.825	1.172
.030	.030	.230	.234	.430	.460	.630	.741	.830	1.188
.035	.035	.235	.239	.435	.466	.635	.750	.835	1.204
.040	.040	.240	.245	.440	.472	.640	.758	.840	1.221
.045	.045	.245	.250	.445	.478	.645	.767	.845	1.238
.050	.050	.250	.255	.450	.485	.650	.775	.850	1.256
.055	.055	.255	.261	.455	.491	.655	.784	.855	1.274
.060	.060	.260	.266	.460	.497	.660	.793	.860	1.293
.065	.065	.265	.271	.465	.504	.665	.802	.865	1.313
.070	.070	.270	.277	.470	.510	.670	.811	.870	1.333
.075	.075	.275	.282	.475	.517	.675	.820	.875	1.354
.080	.080	.280	.288	.480	.523	.680	.829	.880	1.376
.085	.085	.285	.293	.485	.530	.685	.838	.885	1.398
.090	.090	.290	.299	.490	.536	.690	.848	.890	1.422
.095	.095	.295	.304	.495	.543	.695	.858	.895	1.447
.100	.100	.300	.310	.500	.549	.700	.867	.900	1.472
.105	.105	.305	.315	.505	.556	.705	.877	.905	1.499
.110	.110	.310	.321	.510	.563	.710	.887	.910	1.528
.115	.116	.315	.326	.515	.570	.715	.897	.915	1.557
.120	.121	.320	.332	.520	.576	.720	.908	.920	1.589
.125	.126	.325	.337	.525	.583	.725	.918	.925	1.623
.130	.131	.330	.343	.530	.590	.730	.929	.930	1.658
.135	.136	.335	.348	.535	.597	.735	.940	.935	1.697
.140	.141	.340	.354	.540	.604	.740	.950	.940	1.738
.145	.146	.345	.360	.545	.611	.745	.962	.945	1.783
.150	.151	.350	.365	.550	.618	.750	.973	.950	1.832
.155	.156	.355	.371	.555	.626	.755	.984	.955	1.886
.160	.161	.360	.377	.560	.633	.760	.996	.960	1.946
.165	.167	.365	.383	.565	.640	.765	1.008	.965	2.014
.170	.172	.370	.388	.570	.648	.770	1.020	.970	2.092
.175	.177	.375	.394	.575	.655	.775	1.033	.975	2.185
.180	.182	.380	.400	.580	.662	.780	1.045	.980	2.298
.185	.187	.385	.406	.585	.670	.785	1.058	.985	2.443
.190	.192	.390	.412	.590	.678	.790	1.071	.990	2.647
.195	.198	.395	.418	.595	.685	.795	1.085	.995	2.994

SOURCE: Reprinted with permission from Edwards (1967).

because raw data could be retrieved, the overall effect size was based on the cumulation of raw data. For instance, the analysis of the presence versus absence of a monetary incentive on returning the questionnaire found incentives to be superior, with r = +.15.

TABLE 5.6
Example of r-Index Estimation and Tests of Homogeneity

Study	n_i	r_i	z_i	$n_{i.} - 3$	$(n_{i.} - 3)z_i$	$(n_{i.} - 3)z_{i}^2$	Q_b Grouping
1	1,021	.08	.08	1,018	81.44	6.52	A
2	1,955	.27	.28	1,952	546.56	153.04	A
3	12,146	.26	.27	12,143	3278.61	885.22	A
4	3,505	.06	.06	3,502	210.12	12.61	B
5	3,606	.12	.12	3,603	432.36	51.88	B
6	4,157	.22	.22	4,154	913.88	201.05	B
Σ	26,390	.85	.87	26,372	5464.97	1310.32	

$z = 5462.97/26,372 = .207$

$CI_{z.95\%} = .207 \pm \dfrac{1.96}{\sqrt{26,372}} = .207 \pm .012$

$Q_t = 1310.32 - \dfrac{(5462.97)^2}{26,372} = 178.66$

$Q_w = 34.95 + 50.40 = 85.35$

$Q_b = 178.66 - 85.35 = 93.31$

112

ANALYZING VARIANCE IN
EFFECT SIZES ACROSS STUDIES

The analytic procedures described thus far have illustrated how to combine the probabilistic results of separate studies and how to generate an estimate of the strength of relations. Another set of statistical techniques is helpful in discovering why effect sizes vary from one study to another. In these analyses the effect sizes found in the separate studies are the dependent variables and the varying characteristics of the studies are the predictor variables. Thus the reviewer asks whether the magnitude of relation between two variables in a study is affected by the way the study was designed or carried out.

One thing to note about the effect sizes in Tables 5.4 and 5.6 is that the sizes of the effects vary from comparison to comparison. An explanation for this variability is not only important, but it also represents the most unique contribution of the research review. By performing an analysis of differences in effect sizes, the reviewer can gain insight into the factors that affect relationship strengths even though these factors may have never been studied in a single experiment. Assume, for instance, that the first four studies listed in Table 5.4 were conducted in elementary school, and the last three studies were conducted in high school. Is the strength of relation between the two variables different for students at different grades? This question could be tentatively answered through the use of the analytic techniques described below, even though no single study employed both elementary and high school samples.

The techniques that follow are again only a few examples from many procedures for analyzing variance in effects. Their description is conceptual and brief. Those interested in applying the formulas are advised first to examine more detailed treatments, especially those in Hedges and Olkin (1985) or Rosenthal (1984).

Traditional Inference Statistics

The first means for analyzing the variance in effect sizes involves the application of the traditional inference procedures that are employed by primary researchers. Thus if a reviewer of drug treatments of hyperactivity wished to discover whether comparisons using boys revealed stronger or weaker effects than comparisons using girls, he or she might do a t-test on the difference between effect sizes found in comparisons using exclusively boys versus comparisons using exclusively girls. Or if the reviewer were interested in whether the effect size was influenced by the length of delay between treatment and the measurement of hyperactivity, he or she might correlate the length of delay in each comparison with its effect size. In this instance the predictor and dependent variables are continuous, so the significance test associated with the correlation coefficient is the appropriate inferential statistic. For more complex questions a reviewer might categorize effect sizes into multifactor groupings—for instance, according to the gender and age of participants—and perform an analysis of variance or multiple regression on effect sizes. For Table 5.4, if a one-way analysis of variance were conducted comparing the first four d-indexes with the last three d-indexes the result would be nonsignificant.

Standard inference procedures were the techniques initially used by quantitative reviewers for examining variance in effects. Glass et al. (1981) detail how this approach is carried out. However, at least two problems arise with the use of traditional inference procedures in research synthesis. The first is that these procedures do not test the hypothesis that the variability in effect sizes is due solely to sampling error (see the discussion of variability in main effects earlier in this chapter). Therefore, traditional inference procedures can reveal associations between design characteristics and study results without also indicating that the overall variance in effects is no greater than that expected by chance.

Finally, because effect sizes can be based on different numbers of data points (sample sizes), they can have different sampling variances associated with them. If this is the case, the effect sizes violate the assumption of homogeneity of variance that underlies traditional inference tests.

Homogeneity Analyses

A second set of techniques overcome the problems associated with the traditional procedures. Homogeneity statistics ask the question, Is the variance in effect sizes significantly different from that expected by sampling error? If the answer is no, then some methodologists suggest the reviewer might end the analysis there. After all, chance or sampling error is the simplest and most parsimonious explanation. If the answer is yes—that is, if the effect sizes display significantly greater variability than expected by chance—the reviewer then begins to examine other potential sources of variance.

An approach to homogeneity analysis will be described that was introduced simultaneously by Rosenthal and Rubin (1982) and Hedges (1982a). The formula presented by Hedges and Olkin (1985) will be given here and the procedures using d-indexes will be described first.

The d-index. In order to test whether a set of d-indexes is homogeneous, the reviewer must calculate a statistic that Hedges and Olkin (1985) call Q_t:

$$Q_t = \sum_{i=1}^{n} w_i d_i^2 - \left(\sum_{i=1}^{n} w_i d_i \right)^2 / \sum_{i=1}^{n} w_i \qquad [16]$$

where all terms are defined as above.

The Q-statistic has a chi-square distribution with $N - 1$ degrees of freedom, or one less than the number of comparisons. The reviewer refers the obtained value of Q_t to a table of (upper tail) chi-square values. If the obtained value is greater than the critical value for the upper tail of a chi-square at the chosen level of significance, the reviewer rejects the hypothesis that the variance in effect sizes was produced by sampling error alone. Table 5.7 presents the distribution of chi-square for selected probability levels.

For the set of comparisons given in Table 5.4 the value of Q_t equals 4.5. The critical value for chi-square at $p < .05$ based on 6 degrees of freedom is 12.59. Therefore, the hypothesis that sampling error explains the differences in these d-indexes cannot be rejected.

The procedures to test whether a methodological or conceptual distinction between comparisons explains variance in effect sizes involves three steps. First, a Q-statistic is calculated separately for each subgroup of comparisons. For instance, to compare the first four d-indexes in Table 5.4 with the last three, a separate Q-statistic is calculated for each grouping. Then, the values of these Q-statistics are summed to form a value called Q_w. This value is then subtracted from Q_t to obtain Q_b:

$$Q_b = Q_t - Q_w \qquad [17]$$

where all terms are defined as above.

The statistic Q_b is used to test whether the *average* effects of the groupings are homogeneous. It is referred to a chi-square table using as degrees of freedom one less than the number of groupings. If the average d-indexes are homogeneous, then the grouping factor does not explain variance in effects beyond that associated with sampling error. If Q_b exceeds the critical value, then the grouping factor is a significant contributor to variance in effect sizes.

In Table 5.4, the Q_b comparing the first four and last three d-indexes is .98. This result is not significant on 1 degree of freedom.

The r-index. The analogous procedures for performing a homogeneity analysis on r-indexes involves the following formula:

$$Q_t = \sum_{i=1}^{N} (n_{i.} - 3)z_i^2 - \left[\sum_{i=1}^{N} (n_{i.} - 3)z_i \right]^2 / \sum_{i=1}^{N} (n_{i.} - 3) \qquad [18]$$

where all terms are defined as above.

To compare groups of r-indexes, Formula 18 is applied to each grouping separately, and the sum of these results, Q_w, is subtracted from Q_t to obtain Q_b.

The results of a homogeneity analysis using the r-index are presented in Table 5.6. The Q_t value of 178.66 is highly significant, based on a chi-square test with 5 degrees of freedom. While it seems that a range of r-indexes from .08 to .27 is not terribly large, Q_t tells us that, given the sizes of the samples on which these estimates are based, the range is too great to be explained by sampling error alone. Something other than sampling error likely is contributing to the variance in r-indexes.

TABLE 5.7
Critical Values of Chi-Square for Given Probability Levels

df	Upper Tail Probabilities					
	.500	.250	.100	.050	.025	.010
1	.455	1.32	2.71	3.84	5.02	6.63
2	1.39	2.77	4.61	5.99	7.38	9.21
3	2.37	4.11	6.25	7.81	9.35	11.3
4	3.36	5.39	7.78	9.49	11.1	13.3
5	4.35	6.63	9.24	11.1	12.8	15.1
6	5.35	7.84	10.6	12.6	14.4	16.8
7	6.35	9.04	12.0	14.1	16.0	18.5
8	7.34	10.2	13.4	15.5	17.5	20.1
9	8.34	11.4	14.7	16.9	19.0	21.7
10	9.34	12.5	16.0	18.3	20.5	23.2
11	10.3	13.7	17.3	19.7	21.9	24.7
12	11.3	14.8	18.5	21.0	23.3	26.2
13	12.3	16.0	19.8	22.4	24.7	27.7
14	13.3	17.1	21.1	23.7	26.1	29.1
15	14.3	18.2	22.3	25.0	27.5	30.6
16	15.3	19.4	23.5	26.3	28.8	32.0
17	16.3	20.5	24.8	27.6	30.2	33.4
18	17.3	21.6	26.0	28.9	31.5	34.8
19	18.3	22.7	27.2	30.1	32.9	36.2
20	19.3	23.8	28.4	31.4	34.2	37.6
21	20.3	24.9	29.6	32.7	35.5	33.9
22	21.3	26.0	30.8	33.9	36.8	40.3
23	22.3	27.1	32.0	35.2	38.1	41.6
24	23.3	28.2	33.2	36.4	39.4	43.0
25	24.3	29.3	34.4	37.7	40.6	44.3
26	25.3	30.4	35.6	38.9	41.9	45.6
27	26.3	31.5	36.7	40.1	43.2	47.0
28	27.3	32.6	37.9	41.3	44.5	48.3
29	28.3	33.7	39.1	42.6	45.7	49.6
30	29.3	34.8	40.3	43.8	47.0	50.9
40	49.3	45.6	51.8	55.8	59.3	63.7
60	59.3	67.0	74.4	79.1	83.3	88.4
	.500	.750	.900	.950	.975	.990
	Lower Tail Probabilities					

SOURCE: Reprinted with permission from Noether (1971).

Suppose we know that the first three correlations in Table 5.6 are from samples of high school students and the last three are from elementary school students. A homogeneity analysis testing the effect of grade level on the magnitude of r-indexes reveals a Q_b of 93.31. This value is highly significant, based on a chi-square test with 1 degree of freedom. For high school students, the average weighted r-index is .253, while for elementary school students it is

$r = .136$. Thus the grade level of the student is one potential explanation for why the r-indexes vary.

Using computer statistics packages. Calculating average weighted effect sizes and homogeneity statistics by hand is time-consuming and open to error. Conveniently, the major computer statistics packages can be used to do many of the calculations.

The weighting factors for the d-index (w_i) and the r-index ($n_i - 3$) can be generated by having the packages carry out the needed arithmetic calculations and defining these as new variables. The intermediate values can be obtained by further arithmetic definition of new variables and by summing these variables, and the sums can then be (1) used to create new data sets or (2) plugged into the final formulae by hand.

With regard to homogeneity analyses, Hedges and Olkin (1985) note that Q-statistics can be calculated using weighted least squares regression programs. For instance, in the Proc GLM procedure available in Version 5 of SAS, the reviewer simply requests that (1) a multiple regression be conducted using the d-indexes or z-transforms of r-indexes as the dependent variable, (2) the moderating variable of interest be used as the predictor variable, and (3) the appropriate weight be used as a weighting factor (SAS Institute, 1985).

The output of the regression analysis is interpreted as follows. The F-test associated with the model mean square is ignored. The total corrected sums of squares is Q_t. As above, the significance of Q can be found by referring this value to a table of chi-square values (Table 5.7). The model sums of squares is Q_b. It also must be referred to a chi-square table to establish its significance.

Problems in Homogeneity Analysis

The most important problem associated with the use of homogeneity statistics involves their practical application. In many instances the reviewer will be confronted with incomplete data reports, particularly when nonsignificant effects are found. It was suggested above that a conservative procedure was to set these effect sizes at zero. However, if the proportion of assumed zero effects is large but an effect actually exists in the population, greater variance in effect sizes may be estimated using this convention than would be the case if complete information on effect sizes were available. Thus while the assumption that researchers reporting null findings without statistics found effect sized equal to exactly zero will have a conservative impact on combined probabilities and estimates of average effect size, this assumption may lead to larger homogeneity statistics if relations actually exist.

A second problem with homogeneity statistics is that they appear to be low in power. If so, important relations may be missed when homogeneity statistics are used along with conventional levels of statistical significance.

Third, homogeneity statistics can become unreliable and difficult to interpret when the reviewer wishes to test more than one moderator of effect sizes at a time. Hedges and Olkin (1985) present a rigorous model for testing multiple moderators. The model uses sequential tests for homogeneity by removing one at a time variances in effects due to individual moderators. The procedure is often difficult to apply, however, because characteristics of studies are often correlated with one another. For example, suppose it is believed that the effect of homework on achievement is influenced by both the grade level of the student and the level of standardization of the dependent measure. In the comparisons to be analyzed, however, it is found that these two study characteristics are confounded—more studies of high school students used standardized tests, while more studies of elementary school students used class grades. Just as in traditional regression analyses, these intercorrelations make interpretation difficult. In particular, they make the order in which variables are entered into the analysis critical—different orders can result in dramatically different results.

One solution to intercorrelated study characteristics is to generate homogeneity statistics for each characteristic separately, by repeating the calculation of Q-statistics as described above. Then, when the results concerning moderators of effect are interpreted, the reviewer also examines a matrix of intercorrelations among the moderators. This way the reviewer can alert readers to study characteristics that may be confounded and draw inferences with these relations in mind.

A final problem is that the results of homogeneity statistics depend somewhat on the choice of the effect size metric. For instance, the same set of data can yield different results depending on whether d-indexes or r-indexes are used to express relations. This is because d-indexes and r-indexes are not related by a linear transform. The problem of nonequivalent results also appears in primary data analysis; that is, the same data analyzed with parametric and nonparametric statistics can yield different results. However, in primary statistical analyses the differences between one technique and another are well established and the relative appropriateness of one technique or another is fairly easy to evaluate. With the homogeneity statistics these ground rules are not yet clear.

In sum, the quantitative analysis of effect sizes is a new field. Problems in interpretation as well as the precise statistical properties of formulas are still being discovered. While it is clear that a formal analysis of effect sizes should be an integral part of any research review containing large numbers of comparisons, it is also clear that at present reviewers must take great care in the application of these statistics and in the description of how they were applied.

Raw Data Analysis

In instances where raw data from comparisons are available, the moderating hypotheses examined by the homogeneity statistics can be tested by the presence or absence of statistical interactions. That is, the reviewer can perform a mixed-model analysis of variance on the accumulated raw data, using comparison characteristics as between-groups factors and the within-study comparisons as the within-groups factor. If the influence of any within-comparison effect is dependent upon the moderator, it will appear as a significant interaction in the analysis. A significant main effect attributable to research characteristics (the between-groups factor) would indicate that the overall mean on the dependent variable varied from one group of studies to the other. For example, suppose 12 studies of drug treatment effects on children's hyperactivity were found and the raw data from each were available. In addition, assume that 6 of these studies were conducted on boys only and 6 conducted on girls only. The reviewer could conduct an analysis so that drug versus control groups was the within-groups factor and boys versus girls was the between-groups factor. A significant main effect for the drug versus control comparison would indicate study-generated evidence for a drug effect. A significant main effect for gender would indicate that comparisons using one gender revealed greater levels of hyperactivity than comparisons using the other gender. Finally, significant interaction between gender and treatment would indicate that the effect of the drug treatment depended on whether or not the sampled children were boys or girls.

As mentioned above, the practical utility of the raw data analysis is limited both by the infrequency with which raw data can be obtained and by the use of different measurement scales by different researchers.

Variance in Effect Sizes and Review-Generated Evidence

The evidence uncovered through an examination of variance in effect sizes is review-generated evidence, as discussed in Chapter 2. That is, relations between study characteristics and effect sizes cannot be interpreted by the reviewer as uncovering causal relations. As discussed in detail above, in many instances different characteristics of studies will be correlated with one another and it will be impossible to tell which of the correlated characteristics is the true causal agent. Therefore, while review-generated evidence is unique to the research review and represents an important addition to our information about and understanding of research topics, statements of causality based on review-generated evidence are very risky. Typically, when review-generated evidence indicates a relation exists, it is used by the reviewer to point out future fruitful directions for primary researchers.

The illustrative reviews. One of the illustrative reviews, on drug treatments of hyperactivity, employed traditional inference procedures for drawing distinctions in effect size magnitudes. Simple one-way analyses of variance and bivariate correlations were employed. In two of the reviews, on homework and on personality moderators of interpersonal expectancy effects, homogeneity statistics were used. Finally, the review of response rates to questionnaires accumulated raw data. Selected results from these analyses will be presented in the next chapter.

VALIDITY ISSUES IN RESEARCH SYNTHESIS

The first threat to validity arising during the analysis and interpretation stage is that the rules of inference a reviewer employs may be inappropriate. In nonquantitative reviews the appropriateness of inference rules is difficult to assess because the reviewer rarely makes them explicit. In quantitative reviews the suppositions underlying statistical tests are generally known and some statistical biases in reviews can be removed. A complete testing of inference rules may never be possible, but the users of quantitative reviews can decide at least informally whether the statistical assumptions have been met. Regardless of the strategy used, the possibility always exists that the reviewer has used an invalid rule for inferring a characteristic of the target population.

The second threat to validity introduced during analysis and interpretation is that review-generated evidence may be misinterpreted as supporting statements of causality. It has been noted several times in the text that any variable or relation within a review can be examined through either study- or review-generated evidence. However, the scientific status of conclusions based on the different types of evidence can be quite different. Specifically, study-generated evidence is capable of establishing causal precedence among variables, while review-generated evidence is always purely associational.

Protecting Validity

Recommendations about what assumptions are appropriate for reviewers to make about their data will depend on the purposes of a review and the peculiarities of a problem area. This is as true of quantitative procedures as of nonquantitative ones. The only sound general advice is that reviewers should open their rules of inference to public inspection.

(1) Reviewers should be as explicit as possible about their guiding assumptions when they convey their conclusions and inferences to readers.

(2) If there is any evidence bearing on the validity of the interpretation rules, it should be presented. Without this information the reader cannot evaluate the validity of conclusions. Review reports that do not address this issue ought to be considered incomplete.

(3) Reviewers should be careful to distinguish study- and review-generated evidence. Even if the number of studies using each design characteristic is large, the possibility exists that some other unknown methodological feature is correlated with the one involved in an uncovered relation. The more equivocal nature of review-generated inferences means that if this type of evidence indicates that a relation exists, the reviewer should call for the relation to be tested within a single study.

EXERCISES

Study	n_i	z-score (one-tailed)	d_i
1	366	−0.84	−.08
2	96	1.55	.35
3	280	3.29	.47
4	122	0	.00
5	154	1.96	.33
6	120	2.05	.41
7	144	−1.64	−.28

1. What is the combined Z-score and probability level of the seven studies listed above using the Adding Zs method? Using the Adding Weighted Zs method? What is the Fail-safe N?

2. What is the average weighted d-index?

3. Are the effect sizes of the seven studies homogeneous? Calculate your answer both by hand and by using a computer statistical package.

6

The Public Presentation Stage

It is proposed that reviews employ a reporting format similar to primary research reports, including introduction, methods, results, and discussion sections. Special attention is given to discussing how tabulated data can be used in reviews and how effect sizes can be substantively interpreted. Finally, the chapter describes threats to validity that arise from poor reporting and how to protect against them.

Research is complete only when the results are shared with the scientific community. (American Psychological Association, 1983, p. 17)

The translation of an inquirer's notes, printouts, and remembrances into a public document describing the project is a task with profound implications for the accumulation of knowledge. The importance of the public presentation of results is readily acknowledged, but suggestions about how dissemination is best carried out are limited.

REPORT WRITING
IN THE TWO TYPES OF INQUIRY

The codified guidelines for reporting primary research focus mainly on the form of presentation. The American Psychological Association's *Publication Manual* (1983) is quite specific about the style and format of reports. Much less detailed assistance is provided for determining what specific aspects and conclusions of a study the researcher should deem important. For instance, the *Manual* tells researchers to report statistical data and to do so in the results section of the manuscript. However, most researchers perform more statistical tests than they think will interest readers. The *Manual* is much less explicit in guiding judgments about what makes a finding important to readers.

Obviously, the *Manual* is not to be faulted for this omission. Any guidelines for defining the scientific importance of information would need to be separately explicated for a huge array of different topic areas at specific junctures of problem development (Gallo, 1978). Statistical significance cannot be offered as a general guideline, because a null result may be of great interest in some topic areas.

The research reviewer's dilemma is similar in kind to that of the primary researcher, but the dilemma is more dramatic in degree. The reviewer has no formal guidelines similar to the *Publication Manual* that describe how to structure the final report. At best the reviewer follows informal guidelines provided by research reviews on the same or related topics. In most cases the reviewer chooses a format convenient for the particular review problem.

The lack of reporting guidelines for reviewers is a problem because differences in editorial judgments create variance in reviews. This variation is not found in the magnitude or direction of conclusions but in whether particular aspects and results of reviews are included in the report. One reviewer may believe that a methodological characteristic or result of the review would only clutter the manuscript. A second reviewer might think the same piece of information would be of interest to some readers and decide that the "clutter" was worthwhile.

A FORMAT FOR
INTEGRATIVE RESEARCH REVIEW REPORTS

Throughout this book rigorous and systematic rules for conducting primary research have been extended to integrative research reviews. It should not be surprising, then, to find that suggestions concerning the format of integrative review reports draw heavily upon how primary research is currently reported. The basic division of primary research reports into four sections—introduction, methods, results, and discussion—should serve nicely as a structure for integrative reviews. The division of reports into these four sections serves to highlight the types of information that need to be presented in order for readers to evaluate adequately the validity and utility of the review. In the paragraphs that follow, suggestions will be made about some of the information that should be included in integrative research review reports.

The Introduction Section

The introduction to a research review sets the stage for the empirical results that follow. It should contain a conceptual presentation of the research problem and a statement of the problem's significance. In primary research reports, introductions are typically short. Citations are restricted to only a few works closely related to the topic of primary interest. In research reviews introductions should be considerably more exhaustive. Reviewers should attempt to present a complete historical overview of the theoretical and methodological problems associated with the research question. Where do the concepts involved in the research problem come from? Are they grounded in theory, as with the notion of interpersonal expectancy effects, or in practical circumstance, as with the notion of hyperactivity? Are there theoretical debates surrounding the meaning or utility of the concepts? How do the existent theories predict the concepts will be related to one another, and are there conflicting predictions associated with different theories?

The introduction to an integrative research review must carefully contextualize the problem under consideration. Especially when the reviewer intends to apply statistics in the research integration, it is crucial that he or she pay ample attention to the qualitative and historical debates surrounding the research problem. Otherwise, the reviewer will be open to the criticism that numbers have been crunched together without suitable appreciation for the conceptual and theoretical underpinnings that give empirical data their meaning.

As mentioned in Chapter 2, the introduction to an integrative research review is also where the reviewer should discuss previous reviews of the research topic. This review of reviews points out the importance of the new effort and highlights the empirical controversies that the new review hopes to address and resolve.

In sum, the introduction to a research review should present an exhaustive overview of the theoretical and conceptual issues surrounding the research problem and present a general description of prior reviews and the controversies these reviews have created or left unresolved.

The Methods Section

The methods section of an integrative research review will be considerably different from that found in primary research reports, though its purpose is the same: to describe operationally how the inquiry was conducted. Although it is difficult to make general suggestions, most review methods sections will need to address six separate sets of questions.

First, the research reviewer should present the *details of the literature search* itself, including a description of the sources from which studies were retrieved. In addition, when abstract and indexing services and bibliographies are searched, the reviewer needs to report the years covered in them, the keywords that guided the search, and whether manual or computer searches were used, or both. If personal research is included in the review this should be noted as well. Information on the sources, keywords, and coverage of the literature search is perhaps the most crucial aspect of the methods section. It gives the reader the best indication of the extent of the search and therefore how much credibility to place in the conclusions of the review. The description of the literature search tells the reader how different his or her own search of the literature might be. In terms of attempted replication, it is the description of the literature search that is most closely examined when other scholars attempt to understand why different reviews on the same topic area have come to similar or conflicting conclusions.

The second topic that should be addressed in the methods section is the *criteria for relevance* that were applied to the studies uncovered by the literature search. What characteristics of studies were used to determine whether or not a particular effort was relevant to the topic of interest? How many relevance decisions were based on a reading of report titles? On abstracts? On full reports? What characteristics of studies led to exclusion? How many studies were excluded for any given reason? For instance, if a review included only studies that appeared in professional journals, how many potentially relevant but unpublished studies known to the reviewer were excluded?

Of equal importance to a description of excluded studies is a general, qualitative description of the studies that were deemed relevant. For instance, in the review of the effects of drug treatments on childhood hyperactivity, four criteria were met by every study included in the review: (1) the study investigated the effect of drug treatment on children diagnosed as hyperactive; (2) the study employed group comparisons between a drug treatment and control group, a drug and placebo group, and/or a placebo and control group; (3) random assignment was employed as part of the design; and (4) a double-blind procedure was used to administer the treatment and record the dependent variable.

When readers examine the relevance criteria section of a review, they will be critically evaluating the reviewer's notions about how concepts and operations fit together. Much theoretical debate surrounding the outcome of a particular review may focus on how these decisions were made. Some readers may find that relevance criteria were too broad—operational definitions of concepts were included that they feel were irrelevant. This contention can be addressed by employing these distinctions in analyzing potential moderators of research results. Other readers may find the operational definitions were too narrow. This may lead them to examine the results of excluded studies to determine if their results would affect the review's outcome. In general, however, the relevance criteria describe how the reviewer chose to leap from concepts to operations. A detailed description of this procedure will be central to constructive theoretical and conceptual debate concerning the review's outcome.

In addition to this general description of the included evidence, the methods section is a good place for reviewers to describe *prototypical methodologies*. This presentation of prototypes is necessary in research reviews that cover too many studies to examine each one individually. The reviewer should choose several studies that exemplify the methods used by many studies and present the specific details of these research efforts. In instances where only a few studies are found to be relevant, this process may not be necessary—the description of the methods used in a study can be combined with the description of the study's results.

A fourth important topic to be covered in the methods section involves the reviewer's choice of *how independent hypothesis tests were identified*. An explanation of the criteria used to determine whether multiple hypothesis tests from the same report or laboratory were treated as independent or dependent data points should be carefully spelled out.

A fifth subsection of methods should describe the *characteristics of primary research studies* that were retrieved and retained for examination as potential moderators of study outcome. Even if some of these characteristics are not formally tested and are not discussed later in the paper, they should be mentioned. This will alert the reader to characteristics the reviewer might be asked to test at a later date. In other words, the reviewer should fully describe the information about each study that was collected on the coding sheets. In the methods section it is not necessary to describe the frequency with which each retrieved characteristic occurred in the literature; this is best presented in the results section.

A final topic to be addressed in the methods section is that of the *conventions* the reviewer used to facilitate any quantitative analysis of results. Why was a particular effect size metric chosen? Was an adjustment to effect sizes used to remove bias? How were missing outcomes handled? What forms of analyses were chosen to combine results of separate studies and to examine the variability in results across studies? This section should contain a rationale for each choice of conventions and an analysis of what the impact of each choice might be upon the outcomes of the research review.

The Results Section

In the results section, the reviewer presents a summary description of the literature and the statistical basis for any cumulative findings. Thus the results section is where the synthesis of independent studies is described—the evidence that substantiates any inferences about the literature as a whole. While the results sections of reviews will vary considerably depending on the nature of the research topic and evidence, a general strategy for presenting results might divide the section into five subsections.

In the first subsection, the reviewer should tell readers the total number of independent relevant hypotheses tests, along with a breakdown of the sources of these hypotheses tests. For instance, the number of tests found in published versus unpublished reports is sometimes important, as is a description of particular journals that provided large numbers of hypotheses tests. Also, certain descriptive statistics about the literature should be reported. These would include the average or modal date and range of report appearance; the average or modal number of participants sampled in each study, as well as the range of sample sizes; the frequency of studies employing important participant characteristics, such as gender, age, or status differences; and the geographic locations for studies, if relevant. These are but a few of the potential descriptive statistics that might appear at the beginning of a results section.

In general, the first subsection should give the reader a broad quantitative overview of the literature that complements the qualitative overviews contained in the methods and introduction sections. In addition, it should give the reader a sense of the representativeness of the people, procedures, and circumstances contained in the studies. As mentioned in Chapter 3, there is reason to believe that research reviews will pertain more directly to a target population of all individuals and circumstances than will the separate research efforts in the area.

Whatever the outcome of this analysis, this subsection of results allows the reader to access the representativeness of the sampled people and circumstances and therefore the specificity of the review's conclusions.

The second subsection describing results should present the outcomes of combined probability tests covering the relations that were central to the research review. The related Fail-safe Ns should also appear. If any vote counts were done, these should be described.

A third subsection of results should present the effect size analysis. It should begin with a description of the magnitude of the overall effect, the distribution of effect sizes (perhaps presented in graphic form; see Light & Pillemer, 1984), and the 95% confidence interval. The result of the test for homogeneity of the entire set of related effects should also be presented.

A fourth subsection should describe the results of any analyses meant to uncover study characteristics that moderate the size of the effect. For each tested moderator, the reviewer should present the results on whether or not the study characteristic was a significant contributor to variance in effects. If the moderator proved significant, the reviewer should present an average effect size and confidence interval for each grouping of studies.

Finally, the reviewer should devote a subsection to interaction effects found in single studies, if such an analysis is relevant. For instance, Arkin, Cooper, and Kolditz (1980) were interested in summarizing the research on the self-serving bias, that is, on whether individuals assume greater personal responsibility for successful outcomes than for failures. Arkin and colleagues summarized the tests of interactions contained in the covered studies. They found 59 tests for interaction, of which 14 proved significant. These 14 significant interactions were described in a table that contained p-levels and d-indexes associated with each interaction effect and a short description of the interacting third variable. In other reviews other detailed descriptions of the interactions might be warranted, along with quantitative syntheses of the interaction effects.

In sum, the results section should contain the reviewer's overall quantitative description of the covered literature and a report of the relations and moderators of relations that proved significant across studies. This lays the groundwork for the substantive discussion that follows.

The Discussion Section

The discussion section of a research review serves the same functions served by discussions in primary research. First, the reviewer should present a summary of the major results of the review. Then, the reviewer should describe the effect sizes found in the review and interpret their substantive meaning. Next, the reviewer should examine the results of the review in relation to the conclusions of past reviews. Particularly important would be a discussion of how the results of the present review differ from past reviews and why this difference may have occurred. The reviewer also needs to examine the results in relation to the theories and theoretical debates presented in the introduction. If not covered by one of the above suggestions, a discussion of the generality of any findings, as well as limiting conditions that restrict the applicability of any relations, should be included. For instance, if a relation was found between personality and interpersonal expectancy effects, does this hold true for both genders and all situations? Finally, the reviewer should include a discussion of research directions that would be fruitful for future primary research.

In general, then, the discussion section in both primary research and research review is used to make suggestions about the substantive interpretation of relations, the sources and resolution of past controversies, and fruitful directions for future research.

The illustrative reviews. Too much space would be needed to present adequate descriptions of the methods, results, and discussion sections of the illustrative reviews. Also, much of the material contained in the reports has already appeared scattered throughout the book. Selected results will be presented to demonstrate some of the uses of tabulated material in research reviews.

The results of the homework review were presented in a book (Cooper, 1989). Studies comparing homework with no treatment were discussed in one chapter, which began with narrative descriptions of eleven homework versus no-treatment studies conducted before 1962. Effect size estimates were calculated and presented for those studies containing the necessary data, but the effect sizes were not statistically combined.

A table was presented that gave for each study conducted since 1962 the first author, year of publication, and codings on thirteen characteristics. The text gave a summary of the characteristics of the set of studies. These studies were the ones used in the meta-analysis. The text also described one study not used in the meta-analysis because its results could not be transformed into a metric commensurate with the other studies.

A figure was presented that graphically illustrated the distribution of d-indexes. A total of 20 d-indexes were displayed. The text reported that the average d-index was +.21, meaning the average student doing homework had a higher achievement score than 54.7% of students not doing homework. The 95% confidence interval ranged from d = +.13 to d = +.30. Based on the confidence interval, rather than on a combined probability analysis, it was concluded that the difference between the homework and no-treatment conditions was statistically significant.

The significant results from the search for moderators of the homework effect were presented in a table (reproduced here as Table 6.1). Note that the number of comparisons that each test is based on varies for some moderators, due to the use of a shifting unit of analysis. In the text, these results were accompanied by a description of the interrelations among the moderator variables.

The text also contained sections on (1) the effect of homework with third variables controlled, (2) interactions between homework and other variables, and (3) the results of studies examining the effect of homework on attitudes.

TABLE 6.1
Effect Sizes for Comparisons of Homework Versus No Homework on
Measures of Academic Achievement

| | | 95% Confidence Interval | | |
	n	Low Estimate	Mean	High Estimate
Overall ($\chi^2[19] = 57.41$, p < .001)	20	.13	.21	.30
Year ($\chi^2[1] = 8.00$, p < .01)				
1960s	6	.01	.16	.32
1970s	10	.06	.18	.30
1980s	4	.23	.48	.73
Counterbalancing and repeated measures ($\chi^2[1] = 4.68$, p < .05)				
present	4	−.35	−.08	.19
absent	16	.14	.24	.34
Experimenter ($\chi^2[1] = 9.52$, p < .01)				
teacher	8	.25	.41	.57
not teacher	12	.02	.12	.22
Duration of treatment ($\chi^2[1] = 3.89$, p < .05)				
10 weeks	12	.20	.32	.44
more than 10 weeks	8	−.03	.09	.21
Number of assignments($\chi^2[1] = 15.43$, p < .001)				
1-3 per week	14	−.01	.09	.19
4-5 per week	6	.30	.44	.58
Grade ($\chi^2[1] = 3.75$, p < .06)				
4-6	13	.05	.15	.25
7-9	5	.09	.31	.53
10-12	2	.33	.64	.95
Subject matter ($\chi^2[2] = 19.13$, p < .001)				
math	25	.10	.16	.22
reading and English	13	.18	.32	.46
science and social studies	10	.38	.56	.74
Math areas ($\chi^2[3] = 6.79$, p < .01)				
computation	9	.12	.24	.36
concepts	8	.07	.19	.31
problem solving	5	−.12	.02	.16
general or unspecified	3	−.01	.26	.53
Outcome measure ($\chi^2[1] = 6.49$, p < .02)				
class tests or grades	15	.18	.30	.42
standardized tests	5	−.07	.07	.21

SOURCE: Cooper, H. M. (1989). HOMEWORK. Copyright 1989 by Longman Inc. Reprinted by permission.

Finally, the chapter concluded with a summary of results. In a later chapter, the results of the review were compared to other reviews, and implications for policy and future research were discussed.

The results section of the review of personality moderators of interpersonal expectancy effects primarily described the meta-analysis of photo-rating studies. However, the review also contained a description of studies not using the photo-rating situations. In addition to a discussion in the text, a description of these nine studies was presented in tabular form. The table is reproduced here as Table 6.2.

The review of drug treatments of hyperactive children was presented in a very short report, but it still followed the guidelines presented above. The d-indexes from the 61 studies were presented in a figure called a stem-and-leaf display (Tukey, 1977). Figure 6.1 reproduces this display. In a stem-and-leaf display, all of the raw data can be presented in a simple graphic form. The data are first ordered according to magnitude and then the researcher chooses an appropriate number of digits to serve as the stems. The stem-and-leaf display is easier to demonstrate than to describe. For instance, the first column of Figure 6.1 displays the stems, or leading digits, for each of the d-indexes. The second column presents the leaves, or trailing digits, for each of the 16 d-indexes associated with drug versus control comparisons. In this instance, the stems are the first two digits of the d-index (units and tenths) and the leaves are the last digit (hundredths). Thus the smallest d-index uncovered by a drug versus control comparison was .34; the next smallest d-index was .36. A stem-and-leaf display is like a histogram where stems represent intervals and leaves are stacked up to express visually the frequency of intervals. So in the drug versus placebo comparisons (third column), d-indexes most frequently fell between values of .60 and .69, where seven d-indexes can be found. At the bottom of the stem-and-leaf display, information is presented on maximum and minimum values, quartile ranges, and means and standard deviations.

Table 6.3 presents the results of the analyses for the effect of monetary incentives from the review of techniques for increasing response rates to questionnaires. Four cumulative response rates are given. The first rate was called the *experimental* response rate. This was the average response rate for the technique in studies that experimentally manipulated the presence or absence of monetary incentives. The *control* response rate was the average of the control group (no technique) conditions in these experimental studies. The *without control* response rate included response rates from all studies that used monetary incentives but had no control condition. The *absent* response rate was for studies that specifically stated that participants did not receive monetary incentives.

A chi-square test of the frequency of questionnaire responding in studies that experimentally manipulated the presence versus absence of a monetary incentive (i.e., 50.5% for monetary rewards versus 35.2% for no monetary rewards) was highly significant ($\chi^2(1) = 188.1$, p < .0001). This result revealed an r-index

(text continued on page 136)

TABLE 6.2
Personality Moderators of Interpersonal Expectancy Effects: Nonphoto-Rating Studies

Authors	Expectancy Induction/Experimental Task	Personality Variable	Results
Laboratory settings			
Weiss (1969)	Es read instructions to Ss indicating that Ss could expect to overestimate or underestimate the number of dots on tachistoscopically presented slides. A third group of subjects received no expectancy instructions.	Ss' orality/anality	S personality × expectancy interaction *ns*.
Christensen and Rosenthal (1982)	Es led to believe they were about to interview an S of either high or low sociability.	Ss' audio decoding skill	Male Ss who were better decoders detected more bias. No difference for females.
Dusek (1972)	Es led to believe boys would outperform girls on a marble dropping task, or that girls would outperform boys. Ss retrieved marbles from one bin and dropped them through the holes of another bin.	Ss' test anxiety	S personality × bias condition interaction *ns*.
Dana and Dana (1969)	No information concerning expectancy induction. Es administered to Ss the Wechsler Adult Intelligence Scale.	Es' locus of control; Es' susceptibility to influence	E personality × bias interaction *ns* for both personality variables.

Study	Description	Variables	Results
Clark et al. (1976)	Es were led to believe that first 10 taps delivered to an S's Achille's tendon would be heavier or lighter than the next 10 taps. Ss were attached to EEG and EMG recording instruments.	Es' locus of control Ss' locus of control	Significant expectancy × stimulus interval × E personality × S personality interaction for various measures of alpha activity (EEG). Significant expectancy × S personality interaction for a measure of muscle action potential—internal Ss showed effects in the direction of their experimenter's expectancy, external Ss showed effects in the direction opposite to their experimenter's expectancy.
Begum and Shams (1981)	Es were shown data suggesting that some Ss would provide positive color ratings and that other Ss would provide negative ratings. Es then showed colored papers to Ss and asked them to judge the richness of color in the papers.	Es' locus of control Ss' locus of control	E Personality × Expectancy interaction *ns*. S Personality × Expectancy interaction significant—External Ss confirmed their Es expectancies more than Internal Ss.

133

TABLE 6.2 Continued

Authors	Expectancy Induction/Experimental Task	Personality Variable	Results
Instructional settings			
Babad et al. (1982)	Student teachers were led to believe that two of the students in their physical education classes were of "high potential." All students then ran races, performed sit-ups, push-ups, and distance jumps.	Teachers' susceptibility to bias	For sit-up and push-up performance, expectancy × T personality interaction significant—no expectancy effect for low-susceptible teachers, high-expectancy students of high-susceptible teachers outperformed objective expectations (as per an "expected value" for performance calculated by the authors). For distance jumps, expectancy × T personality interacation *ns*. For distance jumps, expectancy × T personality interaction significant—no expectancy effect for low-susceptible teachers, high-expectancy students of high-susceptible teachers outperformed objective expectations.

Therapeutic settings

Bednar and Parker (1969)	Students serving as clients were introduced to "personal growth" counseling by a high-prestige figure who presented information attesting to the validity of the counseling procedures or by a casually dressed research assistant who said nothing about treatment validity.	Clients' susceptibility to bias	Persuasibility and expectancy factors produced no significant effect on therapy-induced behavior change.
Harris and Rosenthal (1986)	Students serving as counselors were told their "clients" (other students) were either extroverted or introverted. Counselors and clients then role-played a peer-counseling session.	Counselors: 16 personality variables measured by the Jackson Personality Research Form; self-monitoring; dogmatism	Significant positive correlations between counselors' ability to bias their clients and counselors' dogmatism, nurturance, and social recognition; significant negative correlation between degree of bias and counselors' impulsivity.
		Clients: 16 personality variables measured by the Jackson Personality Research Form; self-monitoring; dogmatism	Significant positive correlations between clients' susceptibility to bias and clients' self-monitoring and social recognition. Significant negative correlation between degree of bias and clients' social recognition.

Stem	Drug vs Control	Drug vs Placebo	Placebo vs Control	Total[a]
2.1	5			5
2.0		8		8
1.9	4			4
1.8				
1.7	0	24		024
1.6		1		1
1.5	5	0688		05688
1.4	8	126	3	12368
1.3	2	02		022
1.2				
1.1	16	8		168
1.0		8	6	68
.9	39	12399	3	12333999
.8	4	05	9	0549
.7	9	5		59
.6		1125779		1125779
.5	09	07	0	00079
.4		2489		2489
.3	46	168	8	146688
.2		478		478
.1		56		56
.0		005	00000	00000005

Maximum	2.77	2.08	1.43	2.77
Q_3	1.55	1.30	.93	1.30
Median	1.10	.69	.19	.80
Q_1	.59	.42	.00	.38
Minimum	.34	.00	−1.30	−1.30
Mean	1.21	.84	.32	.84
SD	.67	.54	.72	.60

Figure 6.1: d-Indexes for Three Types of Comparisons

SOURCE: Ottenbacher, K. and Cooper, H. Drug treatments of hyperactive children. *Developmental Medicine and Child Neurology*, 1983, *25*, 353-357. Copyright 1983 by Spastics International Medical Publications. Reprinted by permission.

a. Two values, 2.77 and −1.30, are not included in the table.

equal to .15. Further, both prepaid and promised monetary incentives increased responding over no incentive at all (for prepaid, $\chi^2(1) = 145.8$, p < .0001, r = .16; for promised, $\chi^2(1) = 7.5$, p < .01, r = .05). Finally, the amount of the incentive paid appeared to have a strong positive relation to response rates. When the amount offered was correlated with the weighted average response rate, the resulting r-index equaled +.61. It was pointed out, of course, that

TABLE 6.3
Effect of Monetary Incentives on Response Rate

Monetary Incentive	Weighted Average Response Rate	Number of Contacts	Number of Response Rates	SD of Response Rates
Experimental	50.5	5,444	49	20.9
Control	35.2	3,133	30	20.2
Without control	52.2	2,382	15	18.6
Absent	20.1	961	3	21.8
Amount ($)				
0.10	41.6	1,484	17	9.5
0.25	53.9	2,399	10	25.1
0.50	34.7	1,035	9	12.9
1.00	35.9	697	5	19.9
2.00	41.0	200	1	0.0
3.00	40.5	200	1	0.0
5.00	62.1	1,012	13	14.6
10.00	82.0	314	2	5.9
25.00	54.1	205	2	22.5
50.00	75.0	83	1	0.0
Prepaid				
experimental	42.4	3,551	33	18.0
control	26.8	2,271	22	14.6
without control	54.8	1,614	4	29.0
Promised				
experimental	58.6	1,696	13	22.2
control	52.8	796	7	21.9
without control	46.8	768	11	15.1

SOURCE: Yu and Cooper (1983).

researchers should consider the cost/benefit ratio associated with paying extremely large sums of money for responses.

THE SUBSTANTIVE INTERPRETATION OF EFFECT SIZE

In quantitative reviews, one function of a discussion section is the interpretation of the size of the relations. Once the reviewer has generated an effect size, how is he or she to know if it is large or small, meaningful or trivial? Since statistical significance cannot be used as a benchmark—that is, small effects can be statistically significant and large effects nonsignificant—a set of rules must be established for determining the explanatory or practical value of a given effect magnitude.

Cohen (1988) attempts to address the issue of interpreting effect size estimates, and suggests some general definitions for small, medium, and large effect
sizes in the social sciences. However, Cohen chose these quantities to reflect
the typical effect sizes encountered in the behavioral sciences as a whole—he
warns against using his labels to interpret relationship magnitudes within
particular social science disciplines or topic areas. His general labels, however,
illustrate how to go about interpreting effects, and for this purpose they will be
reviewed here.

Cohen labels an effect size small if d = .20 or r = .10. He writes, "Many effects
sought in personality, social, and clinical-psychological research are likely to
be small . . . because of the attenuation in validity of the measures employed
and the subtlety of the issue frequently involved" (p. 13). Large effects, according to Cohen, are frequently "at issue in such fields as sociology, economics,
and experimental and physiological psychology, fields characterized by the
study of potent variables or the presence of good experimental control or both"
(p. 13). Large magnitudes of effect are d = .80 or r = .50. Cohen places medium-
sized effects between these two extremes, that is, d = .50 or r = .30.

Cohen's reasoning can be used to demonstrate the relative nature of effect
sizes. Suppose the review of personality moderators of interpersonal expectancy
effects revealed an average r-index of +.30. How should the relation's magnitude be interpreted? Clearly the interpretation depends on the other relations
chosen as contrasting elements. According to Cohen, this is a medium-sized
behavioral science effect. Thus, compared to other relations in the behavioral
sciences in general, this would be an average effect size, not surprisingly large
or small. However, compared to other personality effects, this effect size may
best be described as large, if we accept Cohen's suggestion that personality
relations are predominantly smaller than r = .30.

Comparing a specific effect to effect sizes found in other disciplines or a
discipline in general may be interesting, but in most instances it is not very
informative. The most informative interpretation occurs when the effect size is
compared to other effects involving the same or similar variables. At the time
Cohen offered his guidelines, holding an effect size in a specialized topic area
up against a criterion as broad as "all behavioral science" might have been the
best contrasting element available. Estimates of average effects for disciplines,
subdisciplines, topic areas, or even single variables or operations were difficult
to find. Today, these calculations are plentiful. Therefore, an effect size should
be labeled "small" or "large" depending on its magnitude relative to a variety
of related estimates. At least some of the contrasting effect sizes should be
closely tied conceptually to the effect found in the specific topic area, involving
the same variables contained in the relation of interest.

In addition to multiple and related choices of contrasting estimates, two other
guides for effect size interpretation may be useful. First, reviewers can assess
how much any relation might be valued by consumers of research. This
assessment involves the difficult problem of making practical judgments about

significance. A hypothetical example will illustrate the point. Suppose a study done in 1970 showed that motorists who regularly checked their tire pressure got 22 miles per gallon of gasoline, while motorists who did not check their tires got 20 miles per gallon. In each group, the standard deviation of the mean was 4 miles per gallon. This indicates that the average motorist driving 10,000 miles a year and buying gas at $.30 a gallon saved 45 gallons of gas and $13.50 annually by checking tire pressure. In terms of the d-index, the pressure checkers and noncheckers were separated by one-half a standard deviation (d = .50), or the average tire checker got better mileage than about 69% of the noncheckers. This effect might have been ignored in 1970. Practically speaking, it might have been considered inconsequential. The same results, however, produced in 1989 with gas costing $1.10 a gallon might elicit a much different reaction. Using 45 gallons less of a scarce resource and saving $49.50 annually would be appreciated by most motorists. Thus the researcher might argue convincingly that the result of the experiment had great practical significance.

If the pressure-checking effect is contrasted with other effects on automobile fuel economy (e.g., tune-ups, observing the speed limit), the comparison might still lead to a conclusion that the effect is small. The researcher, however, can argue that although the effect is of relatively small explanatory value, it may still have great practical significance. This judgment could be justified by arguing that small intervals on the gas usage scale represent large intervals on other, societally-valued indicators—for example, the amount of oil that needs to be imported. Or it might be argued that the cost of implementing a pressure-checking program is relatively inexpensive compared to other interventions. Levin and his colleagues (Levin, 1987; Levin, Glass, & Meister, 1987) have begun to lay out some ground rules for establishing the relative cost-effectiveness of social programs.

A final guide to effect size interpretation that involves research methodology has been alluded to several times in the text. When contrasting effect sizes are chosen, the relative size of effects will reflect not only the explanatory power of the relations but also differences in how data were collected. All else being equal, effect sizes based on studies with strict control over extraneous influences should produce larger effects than less controlled studies (i.e., should have smaller deviations around the mean). For example, a tire pressure-checking effect on gas mileage of d = .50 found in lab tests may be less impressive than a similar finding obtained under normal driving conditions. Effect sizes will also be a function of the strength of the manipulation (for example, the degree of tire underinflation in unchecked cars), the sensitivity of the measures (for example, counting the number of fill-ups versus the number of gallons used), and any restrictions on participant populations (for example, all cars versus only new cars). These illustrations point out only a few methodological considerations that can influence effect size interpretation.

Finally, it should be kept in mind that effect size estimates reported in research reviews are influenced not only by the methodology of the studies reviewed but also by the methodology of the review itself. As Cooper and Arkin (1981) point out:

> If an unbiased inference is to be made from the effect size estimate, it is that other literature reviews using similar retrieval procedures should expect to uncover similar ES's. Researchers . . . [and] policymakers . . . need to adjust ES estimates dependent upon whatever sources of bias (with whatever impact) they feel may have been present in the particular literature search. (p. 227)

Thus it may not be appropriate to assume that the effect size uncovered in a research review is equal to the effect found in the population. The reviewer must determine if the estimate is potentially inflated by an inability to uncover small effect sizes due to bias in the publication process or the literature search.

In sum, Cohen's (1988) labels give only the broadest interpretive yardstick for effect sizes. The most meaningful interpretation of an effect size comes from comparisons to other magnitudes of relation chosen because of their substantive relevance to the topic under study. Complementing this interpretation should be an assessment of the practical value of any explanation and the role of methodology in shaping the conclusion.

The illustrative reviews. The two best examples of how relationship strengths can be interpreted come from the reviews on homework and on questionnaire responding. For homework, it will be recalled that the average d-index of the difference in achievement between students doing homework and students doing no homework was d = +.21. Is this a small or large effect? To help answer this question, the results of other meta-analyses were examined. These were listed in a table, reproduced here as Table 6.4. The eleven meta-analyses contained in the table all examined the effect of instructional strategies or teaching skills on measures of achievement. They were taken from a chapter on research synthesis appearing in the *Handbook of Research on Teaching* (Walberg, 1986).

Based on a comparison with the entries in the table, it was concluded that the effect of homework on achievement can best be described as *above average*. The median effect size in the table is d = +.10, half the size of the homework effect. The relative quality of methods in the different topic areas was also considered. It was assumed that the trustworthiness of the measures of achievement used in the different areas and the soundness of the research designs were roughly equivalent. However, some of the assumptions on which effect size estimates were based were probably more conservative in the homework review than in other reviews. Finally, the practical value of homework was assessed by comparing the relative costs of implementing the different instructional and teaching treatments. Homework can be regarded as a low-cost treatment, especially in comparison with special-class placement and individualized and programmed instruction.

In the review of questionnaire responding, the relative effects of the dozen research design methods were evaluated in comparison to one another, instead

TABLE 6.4
Selected Effect Sizes from Meta-Analysis Examining
Influences on Achievement[a]

Authors (Year)	Independent Variable	Effect Size[b]
Bangert et al. (1981)	individualized versus conventional teaching	+.10
Carlberg and Kavale (1980)	special- versus regular-class placement	−.12
Johnson et al. (1981)	cooperative versus competitive learning	+.78
Kulik and Kulik (1981)	ability grouping	+.10
Kulik et al. (1982)	programmed instruction	+.08
Luiten, Ames, and Aerson (1980)	advance organizers	.23
Pflaum et al. (1980)	direct instruction	.60
Redfield and Rousseau (1981)	higher cognitive questions	.73
Wilkinson (1980)	praise	+.08
Williams et al. (1982)	amount of television watching	+.10
Willson and Putnam (1982)	pretests	+.17

SOURCE: Cooper, H. M. (1989). HOMEWORK. Copyright 1989 by Longman Inc. Reprinted by permission.
a. Topics are those listed by Walberg (1986) as involving achievement as the dependent variable.
b. Effect sizes are expressed in d-indexes.

of separately. Thus the contrasting elements were contained in the review itself. For instance, the r-index of +.16 associated with prepaid monetary incentives was compared with the r-index of +.05 for promised monetary incentives. This was done so that those administering the questionnaire in the future could determine which design characteristics would produce the greatest increase in responding relative to the cost involved in employing that procedure.

VALIDITY ISSUES IN REPORT WRITING

The two threats to validity accompanying report writing relate to the different target populations of the review. First, the omission of details about how the review was conducted is a potential threat to validity. As with primary research, an incomplete report reduces the replicability of the review conclusion. Jackson (1980) examined 36 reviews and found "complete" to be a far-from-accurate description of most reviews:

Only one of the 36 articles reported the indexes and information retrieval systems used to search for primary studies on the topic. Only three of the 36 reported the bibliographies used as a means of locating studies. Only seven indicated whether or not they analyzed the full set of located studies on the topic, instead of some subset. Only one-half of the 36 reported the direction and magnitude of the findings of any of the reviewed primary studies, and few did this for each finding. In addition, very few review articles systematically reported characteristics of the primary research that may have affected the findings. (pp. 456-457)

Without these details, the reader cannot ascertain whether or not a personal review of the literature would lead to similar findings.

The second validity threat in report writing involves the omission of evidence about moderators of relations that other inquirers may find important. Matheson, Bruce, and Beauchamp (1978) observe that "as research on a specific behavior progresses, more details concerning the experimental conditions are found to be relevant" (p. 265). Thus a review will lose its timeliness if the reviewer is not astute enough to identify the variables and moderators that are (or will be) important to an area. More complete reviews will take longer to be replaced by newer reviews, and will therefore have greater temporal generality.

Protecting validity. Recommendations about how reviewers can protect against these threats to validity are as difficult to offer as recommendations for how primary researchers should approach this stage of inquiry. This chapter is filled with suggestions that might provide a starting point. However, reviewers will never be able to predict perfectly which omitted characteristic or result of their reviews will eventually render their conclusions invalid or obsolete. On the positive side, reviewers certainly want their documents to have long lives. We can anticipate that reviewers give considerable thought to how to present the most exhaustive report in the most readable manner.

EXERCISES

1. Read two integrative research reviews. Outline what the authors tell about each of the following: (a) how the literature search was conducted, (b) what rules were used to decide if studies were relevant to the hypothesis, and (c) what rules were used to decide if cumulative relations existed.

2. Find two primary research reports on the same topic that vary in method. Calculate the effect size reported in each. Compare the effect sizes to one another, taking into account the influence of the different methods. Using other criteria, decide whether you consider each effect size large, medium, or small. Justify your decision.

7

Conclusion

This chapter presents general issues pertaining to how the notion of rigorous research reviewing is likely to evolve in the future as well as some considerations surrounding the feasibility of conducting reviews that meet rigorous criteria. Several issues concerning research reviewing and the philosophy of science are also discussed.

There are several issues related to research reviewing that cannot be placed easily into the packaging of events represented by the five-stage model. These overarching considerations deal with problems and promises in applying the guidelines set forth in the previous chapters.

VALIDITY ISSUES REVISITED

First, the five stages of reviewing contained eleven threats to validity. It is likely that other threats exist that have been overlooked in this treatment. Campbell and Stanley's (1963) list of validity threats to primary research was expanded by Campbell (1969), Bracht and Glass (1968), and Cook and Campbell (1979). This same expansion and respecification of threats to validity is also likely to occur in the area of research reviewing. It shows progress in the systematization of issues surrounding legitimate scientific inference.

Several of the threats to validity arising in the course of research reviewing are simply holdovers that represent pervasive problems in primary research. For instance, during data collection it was asserted that a threat to the validity of a review was that people contained in the covered studies might not be representative of the target population. This suggests that any threat associated with a particular primary research design is applicable to a review if the design represents a substantial portion of the covered research. In the examination of review-generated evidence, research designs should be carefully examined as potential moderators of study results. The creation of these "nomological nets" (Cronbach & Meehl, 1955) can be one of the research review's most valuable contributions. However, if an assortment of research designs is not contained in a review, then threats associated with the dominant designs also threaten the review's conclusions.

FEASIBILITY AND COST

It will be considerably more expensive for inquirers to undertake reviews using the guidelines set forth in this book than to conduct reviews in the traditional manner. Money is needed to conduct computer searches and to pay data collectors. Hours are needed to develop evaluative criteria and coding frames and to run analyses. Probably more than one person should be involved, at least in the data evaluation stage.

Should a potential reviewer with limited resources be discouraged from undertaking a project? Certainly not. Just as the perfect, irrefutable primary study has never been conducted, the perfect review remains an ideal. As much as the suggestions of this book have been presented as guidelines for conducting reviews, they are also presented as yardsticks for evaluating reviews. In fact, the reader should be aware of several instances in which the illustrative research reviews fell short of complete adherence to the abstract guidelines. Sacks, Berrier, Reitman, Ancona-Berk, and Chalmers (1987) surveyed 86 meta-analyses and concluded that there was an urgent need for improved methods. A potential reviewer should not hold the guidelines as absolute criteria that must be met, but rather as targets that help the reviewer refine the proposed procedures and breadth of a review until a good balance between rigor and feasibility is struck.

THE SCIENTIFIC METHOD AND DISCONFIRMATION

While the pragmatics of conducting research reviews may mean the inquirer must settle for a less-than-perfect product, this does not mean that the ideals of science need not be strictly applied to the research review process. The crucial scientific element that has been missing from traditional reviewing procedures has been the potential for the disconfirmation of the reviewer's prior beliefs. In most instances, primary researchers undertake their work with some recognition that the results of their study may alter their belief system. Not so the traditional reviewer. By extending the scientific method to research reviews, the reviewer accepts the potential for disconfirmation. Ross and Lepper (1980) state this position nicely:

> We know all too well that the scientific method is not immune to the diseases of biased assimilation, causal explanation, and a host of other nagging afflictions; scientists can be blind, sometimes deliberately so, to unanticipated or uncongenial interpretations of their data and recalcitrant in their theoretical allegiances. . . . Nevertheless, it is the scientific method . . . that has often been responsible for increasing human understanding of the natural and social world. Despite its flaws, it remains the best means of delivering us from the errors of intuitive beliefs and intuitive methods for testing those beliefs. (p. 33)

SCIENTIFIC RESEARCH REVIEWING
AND CREATIVITY

One objection to the introduction of systematic guidelines for research reviews is that such a systematization will stifle creativity. Critics who raise this issue think the rules for conducting and reporting primary research are a "straitjacket" on innovative thinking. I cannot disagree more. Rigorous criteria will not produce reviews that are mechanical and uncreative. The expertise and intuition of the reviewer will be challenged to capitalize on or create opportunities to obtain, evaluate, and analyze information unique to each problem area. I hope the illustrative reviews have demonstrated the diversity and complexity of issues that confront reviewers who adopt the scientific method. These challenges are *created* by scientific rules.

CONCLUSION

This book began with the supposition that research reviewing was a data-gathering exercise that needed to be evaluated against scientific criteria. Because of the growth in empirical research, the increased access to information, and the new techniques for research synthesis, the conclusions of research reviews will become less and less trustworthy unless something is done to systematize the process and make it more rigorous. It is hoped that the concepts presented here have convinced readers that it is feasible and desirable for social scientists to require more rigorous reviews, with greater potential for creating consensus among scholars and for focusing discussion on specific and testable areas of disagreement when conflict does exist. Because of the increasing role that research reviews play in our definition of knowledge, these adjustments in procedures are inevitable if social scientists hope to retain their claim to objectivity.

REFERENCES

American Psychological Association. (1983). *Publication manual* (3rd ed.). Washington, DC: Author.

Arkin, R., Cooper, H., & Kolditz, T. (1980). A statistical review of the literature concerning the self-serving attribution bias in interpersonal influence situations. *Journal of Personality, 48*, 435-448.

Barber, T. (1978). Expecting expectancy effects: Biased data analyses and failure to exclude alternative interpretations in experimenter expectancy research. *Behavioral and Brain Sciences, 3*, 388-390.

Barnett, V., & Lewis, T. (1978). *Outliers in statistical data.* New York: John Wiley.

Bar-Tal, D., & Bar Zohar, Y. (1977). The relationship between perception of locus of control and academic achievement. *Contemporary Educational Psychology, 2*, 181-199.

Bem, D. (1967). Self-perception: An alternative interpretation of cognitive dissonance phenomena. *Psychological Review, 74*, 183-200.

Borchardt, D., & Francis, R. (1984). *How to find out in psychology.* Oxford: Pergamon.

Boyce, B., & Banning, C. (1979). Data accuracy in citation studies. *RQ, 18*(4), 349-350.

Bracht, G., & Glass, G. (1968). The external validity of experiments. *American Educational Research Journal, 5*, 437-474.

Bradley, J. (1981). Pernicious publication practices. *Bulletin of Psychonomic Society, 18*, 31-34.

Campbell, D. (1969). Reforms as experiments. *American Psychologist, 24*, 409-429.

Campbell, D., & Stanley, J. (1963). *Experimental and quasi-experimental designs for research.* Chicago: Rand McNally.

Carlsmith, J., Ellsworth, P., & Aronson, E. (1976). *Methods of research in social psychology.* Reading, MA: Addison-Wesley.

Carlson, M., & Miller, N. (1987). Explanation of the relation between negative mood and helping. *Psychological Bulletin, 102*, 91-108.

Cicchetti, D., & Eron, L. (1979). The reliability of manuscript reviewing for the *Journal of Abnormal Psychology 1979. Proceedings of the American Statistical Association* (Social Statistics Section), *22*, 596-600.

Cohen, J. (1988). *Statistical power analysis for the behavioral sciences* (2nd ed.). Hillsdale, NJ: Lawrence Erlbaum.

Cook, T., & Campbell, D. (1979). *Quasi-experimentation.* Chicago: Rand McNally.

Cook, T., & Leviton, L. (1981). Reviewing the literature: A comparison of traditional methods with meta-analysis. *Journal of Personality, 48*, 449-471.

Cooper, H. (1979). Statistically combining independent studies: A meta-analysis of sex differences in conformity research. *Journal of Personality and Social Psychology, 37*, 131-146.

Cooper, H. (1983). Methodological determinants of outcomes of synthesis of research literature. In P. Wortman (Chair), *An analysis of methodologies used in synthesizing research on desegregation and student achievement.* Symposium conducted at the annual meeting of the American Educational Research Association, Montreal.

Cooper, H. (1986). On the social psychology of using research reviews: The case of desegregation and black achievement. In R. Feldman (Ed.), *The social psychology of education.* Cambridge: Cambridge University Press.

Cooper, H. (1987). Literature searching strategies of integrative research reviewers: A first survey. *Knowledge, 8*, 372-383.

Cooper, H. (1988). The structure of knowledge synthesis: A taxonomy of literature reviews. *Knowledge in Society, 1*, 104-126.

Cooper, H. (1989). *Homework.* New York: Longman.

Cooper, H., & Arkin, R. (1981). On quantitative reviewing. *Journal of Personality, 49*, 225-230.

Cooper, H., Burger, J., & Good, T. (1981). Gender differences in the academic locus of control beliefs of young children. *Journal of Personality and Social Psychology, 40*, 562-572.

Cooper, H., & Hazelrigg, P. (1988). Personality moderators of interpersonal expectancy effects: An integrative research review. *Journal of Personality and Social Psychology*.

Cooper, H., & Ribble, R. (in press). Influences on the outcome of literature searches for integrative research reviews. *Knowledge: Creation, Diffusion, Utilization*.

Cooper, H., & Rosenthal, R. (1980). Statistical versus traditional procedures for summarizing research findings. *Psychological Bulletin, 87*, 442-449.

Crandall, V., Katkovsky, W., & Crandall, V. (1965). Children's beliefs in their own control of reinforcement in intellectual-academic achievement situations. *Child Development, 36*, 91-109.

Crane, D. (1969). Social structure in a group of scientists: A test of the "invisible college" hypothesis. *American Sociological Review, 34*, 335-352.

Cronbach, H., & Meehl, P. (1955). Construct validity in psychological tests. *Psychological Bulletin, 52*, 281-302.

Cuadra, C., & Katter, R. (1967). Opening the black box of relevance. *Journal of Documentation, 23*, 291-303.

Davidson, D. (1977). The effects of individual differences of cognitive style on judgements of document relevance. *Journal of the American Society for Information Science, 8*, 273-284.

Edwards, A. L. (1967). *Statistical methods* (2nd ed.). New York: Holt, Rinehart & Winston.

Eysenck, H. (1978). An exercise in mega-silliness. *American Psychologist, 33*, 517.

Feinberg, R. (1981). Positive side effects of on-line information retrieval. *Teaching of Psychology, 8*, 51-52.

Festinger, L., & Carlsmith, B. (1959). Cognitive consequences of forced compliance. *Journal of Abnormal and Social Psychology, 58*, 203-210.

Findley, M., & Cooper, H. (1981). A comparison of introductory social psychology textbook citations in five research areas. *Personality and Social Psychology Bulletin, 7*, 173-176.

Findley, M., & Cooper, H. (1983). Locus of control and academic achievement: A literature review. *Journal of Personality and Social Psychology, 44*, 419-427.

Fisher, R. (1932). *Statistical methods for research workers*. London: Oliver & Boyd.

Friedman, H. (1968). Magnitude of experimental effect and a table for its rapid estimation. *Psychological Bulletin, 70*, 245-251.

Gallo, P. (1978). Meta-analysis: A mixed meta-phor? *American Psychologist, 33*, 515-517.

Garvey, W., & Griffith, B. (1971). Scientific communications: Its role in the conduct of research and creation of knowledge. *American Psychologist, 26*, 349-361.

Glass, G. (1976). Primary, secondary, and meta-analysis of research. *Educational Researcher, 5*, 3-8.

Glass, G. (1977). Integrating findings: The meta-analysis of research. In *Review of research in education* (Vol. 5). Itasca, IL: F. E. Peacock.

Glass, G., McGaw, B., & Smith, M. (1981). *Meta-analysis in social research*. Beverly Hills, CA: Sage.

Glass, G., & Smith, M. (1978). Reply to Eysenck. *American Psychologist, 33*, 517-518.

Gottfredson, S. (1978). Evaluating psychological research reports. *American Psychologist, 33*, 920-934.

Gover, H. (1983). *Keys to library research on the graduate level: A guide to guides*. Lanham, MD: University Press of America.

Greenberg, J., & Folger, R. (1988). *Controversial issues in social research methods*. New York: Springer-Verlag.

Greenwald, A. (1975). Consequences of prejudices against the null hypothesis. *Psychological Bulletin, 82*, 1-20.

Griffith, B., & Mullins, N. (1972). Coherent social groups in scientific change. *Science, 177,* 959-964.

Guzzo, R., Jackson, S., & Katzell, R. (1987). Meta-analysis analysis. In B. Staw & L. Cummings (Eds.), *Research in organizational behavior* (Vol. 9). Greenwich, CT: JAI.

Harper, R., Weins, A., & Matarazzo, J. (1978). *Nonverbal communication: The state of the art.* New York: John Wiley.

Hedges, L. (1980). Unbiased estimation of effect size. *Evaluation in Education: An International Review Series, 4,* 25-27.

Hedges, L. (1982a). Estimation of effect size from a series of independent experiments. *Psychological Bulletin, 92,* 490-499.

Hedges, L. (1982b). Fitting categorical models to effect sizes from a series of experiments. *Journal of Educational Statistics, 7*(2), 119-137.

Hedges, L., & Olkin, I. (1980). Vote-counting methods in research synthesis. *Psychological Bulletin, 88,* 359-369.

Hedges, L., & Olkin, I. (1985). *Statistical methods for meta-analysis.* Orlando, FL: Academic Press.

Hunter, J., Schmidt, F., & Jackson, G. (1982). *Meta-analysis: Cumulating research findings across studies.* Beverly Hills, CA: Sage.

Institute for Scientific Information. (1980). *Social Sciences Citation Index.* Philadelphia: Author.

Jackson, G. (1980). Methods for integrative reviews. *Review of Educational Research, 50,* 438-460.

Kanuk, L., & Berensen, C. (1975). Mail surveys and response rates: A literature review. *Journal of Marketing Research, 12,* 440-453.

Katz, W. (1987). *Introduction to reference work* (Vol. 2). New York: McGraw-Hill.

Kazdin, A., Durac, J., & Agteros, T. (1979). Meta-meta analysis: A new method for evaluating therapy outcome. *Behavioral Research and Therapy, 17,* 397-399.

Kerlinger, F. (1973). *Foundations of behavioral research* (2nd ed.). New York: Holt, Rinehart & Winston.

Lane, D., & Dunlap, W. (1978). Estimating effect sizes: Bias resulting from the significance criterion in editorial decisions. *British Journal of Mathematical and Statistical Psychology, 31,* 107-112.

Levin, H. (1987). Cost-benefit and cost-effectiveness analysis. *New Directions for Program Evaluation, 34,* 83-99.

Levin, H., Glass, G., & Meister, G. (1987). Cost-effectiveness and computer-assisted instruction. *Evaluation Review, 11,* 50-72.

Light, R., & Pillemer, D. (1984). *Summing up: The science of reviewing research.* Cambridge, MA: Harvard University.

Lipsey, H. (in press). *Design sensitivity: Statistical power for detecting the effects of interventions.* Newbury Park, CA: Sage.

Lord, C., Ross, L., & Lepper, M. (1979). Biased assimilation and attitude polarization: The effects of prior theories on subsequently considered evidence. *Journal of Personality and Social Psychology, 37,* 2098-2109.

Lykken, D. (1968). Statistical significance in psychological research. *Psychological Bulletin, 70,* 151-159.

Maccoby, E., & Jacklin, C. (1974). *The psychology of sex differences.* Stanford, CA: Stanford University Press.

Mahoney, M. (1977). Publication prejudices: An experimental study of confirmatory bias in the peer review system. *Cognitive Therapy and Research, 1,* 161-175.

Mansfield, R., & Bussey, T. (1977). Meta-analysis of research: A rejoinder to Glass. *Educational Researcher, 6,* 3.

Marsh, H., & Ball, S. (1981). Interjudgmental reliability of reviews for the *Journal of Educational Psychology*. *Journal of Educational Psychology, 73*, 872-880.

Matheson, D., Bruce, R., & Beauchamp, K. (1978). *Experimental psychology*. New York: Holt, Rinehart & Winston.

McClellend, C., Atkinson, J., Clark, R., & Lowel, E. (1953). *The achievement motive*. New York: Appleton-Century-Crofts.

McNemar, Q. (1946). Opinion-attitude methodology. *Psychological Bulletin, 43*, 289-374.

Menzel, H. (1966). Scientific communication: Five themes from sociology. *American Psychologist, 21*, 999-1004.

Mosteller, F., & Bush, R. (1954). Selected quantitative techniques. In G. Lindzey (Ed.), *Handbook of social psychology: Vol. 1. Theory and method*. Cambridge, MA: Addison-Wesley.

Noether, G. (1971). *Introduction to statistics: A fresh approach*. Boston: Houghton Mifflin.

Nunnally, J. (1960). The place of statistics in psychology. *Education and Psychological Measurement, 20*, 641-650.

Oakes, M. (1986). *Statistical inference: A commentary for the social and behavioural sciences*. Chichester: John Wiley.

Ottenbacher, K., & Cooper, H. (1983). Drug treatments of hyperactivity in children. *Developmental Medicine and Child Neurology, 25*, 353-357.

Pearson, K. (1933). On a method of determining whether a sample of size n supposed to have been drawn from a parent population having a known probability integral has probably been drawn at random. *Biometrika, 25*, 379-410.

Peters, D., & Ceci, S. (1982). Peer-review practices of psychological journals: The fate of published articles, submitted again. *Behavioral and Brain Sciences, 5*, 187-255.

Presby, S. (1978). Overly broad categories obscure important differences between therapies. *American Psychologist, 33*, 514-515.

Price, D. (1965). Networks of scientific papers. *Science, 149*, 510-515.

Price, D. (1966). Collaboration in an invisible college. *American Psychologist, 21*, 1011-1018.

Raudenbush, S., Becker, B., & Kalain, H. (1988). Modeling multivariate effect sizes. *Psychological Bulletin, 103*, 111-120.

Raudenbush, S., & Bryk, A. (1985). Empirical Bayes meta-analysis. *Journal of Educational Statistics, 10*, 75-98.

Reed, J., & Baxter, P. (1983). *Library use: A handbook for psychology*. Washington, DC: American Psychological Association.

Reynolds, P. (1971). *A primer in theory construction*. Indianapolis: Bobbs-Merrill.

Rosenthal, R. (1976). *Experimenter effects in behavioral research*. New York: Appleton-Century-Crofts.

Rosenthal, R. (1978a). How often are our numbers wrong? *American Psychologist, 33*, 1005-1008.

Rosenthal, R. (1978b). Combining results of independent studies. *Psychological Bulletin, 85*, 185-193.

Rosenthal, R. (1979a). The "file drawer problem" and tolerance for null results. *Psychological Bulletin, 86*, 638-641.

Rosenthal, R. (1979b). Replications and their relative utility. *Replications in Social Psychology, 1*, 15-23.

Rosenthal, R. (1980). Summarizing significance levels. *New Directions for Methodology of Social and Behavioral Science, 5*, 33-46.

Rosenthal, R. (1982). Valid interpretation of quantitative research results. *New Directions for Methodology of Social and Behavioral Science, 12*, 59-75.

Rosenthal, R. (1984). *Meta-analytic procedures for social research*. Beverly Hills, CA: Sage.

Rosenthal, R., & Rubin, D. (1982). Comparing effect sizes of independent studies. *Psychological Bulletin, 92*, 500-504.

Ross, L., & Lepper, R. (1980). The perseverance of beliefs: Empirical and normative considerations. *New Directions for Methodology of Social and Behavioral Science, 4,* 17-36.

Rotter, J. (1954). *Social learning and clinical psychology.* Englewood Cliffs, NJ: Prentice-Hall.

Sacks, H., Berrier, J., Reitman, D., Ancona-Berk, V., & Chalmers, T. (1987). Meta-analysis of randomized controlled trials. *New England Journal of Medicine, 316,* 450-455.

Saracevic, T. (1970). The concept of "relevance" in information science: A historical review. In T. Saracevic (Ed.), *Introduction to information science.* New York: Bowker.

SAS Institute. (1985). *SAS user's guide: Statistics* (Version 5). Cary, NC: Author.

Scarr, S., & Weber, B. (1978). The reliability of reviews for the *American Psychologist. American Psychologist, 33,* 935.

Scholarly communication: Report of the national enquiry. (1979). Baltimore: Johns Hopkins University Press.

Selltiz, C., Wrightsman, L., & Cook, S. (1976). *Research methods in social relations* (3rd ed.). New York: Holt, Rinehart & Winston.

Simon, J. (1978). *Basic research methods in social science* (2nd ed.). New York: Random House.

Smith, M. (1980). Publication bias and meta-analysis. *Evaluation in Education: An International Review Series, 4,* 22-24.

Smith, M., & Glass, G. (1977). Meta-analysis of psychotherapy outcome studies. *American Psychologist, 32,* 752-760.

Stoan, S. (1982). Computer searching: A primer for uninformed scholars. *Academe, 68,* 10-15.

Stock, W., Okun, M., Haring, M., Miller, W., Kinney, C., & Ceurvorst, R. (1982). Rigor and data synthesis: A case study of reliability in meta-analysis. *Educational Researcher, 11*(6), 10-14.

Taveggia, T. (1974). Resolving research controversy through empirical cumuation. *Sociological Methods and Research, 2,* 395-407.

Tukey, J. (1977). *Exploratory data analysis.* Reading, MA: Addison-Wesley.

Viana, M. (1980). Statistical methods for summarizing independent correlational results. *Journal of Educational Statistics, 5,* 83-104.

Walberg, H. (1986). Synthesis of research on teaching. In M. Wittrock (Ed.), *Handbook of research on teaching* (3rd ed.). New York: Macmillan.

Webb, E., Campbell, D., Schwartz, R., Sechrest, L., & Grove, J. (1981). *Nonreactive measures in the social sciences.* Boston: Houghton Mifflin.

White, C. (1986). *Sources of information in the social sciences.* Chicago: American Library Association.

Whitehurst, G. (1984). Interrater agreement for journal manuscript reviews. *American Psychologist, 39, 22-28.*

Williams, B. (1978). *A sampler on sampling.* New York: John Wiley.

Wolins, L. (1962). Responsibility for raw data. *American Psychologist, 22,* 657-658.

Xhignesse, L., & Osgood, C. (1967). Bibliographical citation characteristics of the psychological journal network in 1950 and 1960. *American Psychologist, 22,* 779-791.

Yu, J., & Cooper, H. (1983). A quantitative review of research design effects on response rates to questionnaires. *Journal of Marketing Research, 20,* 36-44.

Zuckerman, M., DePaulo, B., & Rosenthal, R. (1981). Verbal and nonverbal communication of deception. In *Advances in experimental social psychology* (Vol. 14). New York: Academic Press.

AUTHOR INDEX

SUBJECT INDEX

ABOUT THE AUTHOR

Harris M. Cooper is Professor of Psychology and Research Associate of the Center for Research in Social Behavior at the University of Missouri—Columbia. He has also taught at Colgate University, and has been a Postdoctoral Fellow at Harvard University, a Visiting Scholar at Stanford University, and a Visiting Professor at the University of Oregon. He has published articles on numerous facets of research reviewing and has conducted nearly two dozen substantive reviews. He is a member of the Advisory Committee of the Russell Sage Foundation's Program on Research Synthesis and an advising editor for four journals in psychology and education. He was the first recipient of the American Educational Research Association's Raymond B. Cattell Early Career Award for Programmatic Research.

NOTES

NOTES